Republic F Thunderchief
Peacetime Operations

THEO VAN GEFFEN AND
CMSGT GERALD ARRUDA (USAF, RET.)

Books

HISTORIC MILITARY AIRCRAFT SERIES, VOLUME 6

Front cover image: An F-105B Thunderchief of the 335th Tactical Fighter Squadron near Eglin Air Force Base (AFB), Florida. (RAC/CAM)

Back cover image: Three F-105Ds of the 466th Tactical Fighter Squadron/419th Tactical Fighter Wing at Hill Air Force Base, Utah, on the way back from a bombing/gunnery mission on Eagle Range, west of Salt Lake City. (TvG)

Title page image: F-105D 62-4279 of Yellow Section (12th TFS/18th TFW) in flight near its home station Kadena Air Base on Okinawa. (Dag Damewood)

Contents page image: Eglin 1-62 was a highly concentrated four-hour USAF demonstration at Eglin AFB, performed on May 4, 1962, for President John Kennedy, Vice President Lyndon Johnson and other government leaders. The 333rd and 335th TFS/4th TFW at Seymour Johnson AFB participated with 33 F-105Ds. The photo shows at least 19 of them at the Eglin flight line. (RAC/CAM)

Authors' Note

The history of the F-105 Thunderchief and the units it was assigned to is a rather complicated and extensive one. No book has yet been published that tells the complete story. Neither this book nor Part Two (which will deal with the war in Southeast Asia) will either. We, after discussion with the publisher, decided to focus on a couple of specific subjects, so that they at least come close to an almost complete coverage. The general photos will tell the rest of the story.

Acknowledgements

Special thanks go to Sandor Kocsis, the 419th Tactical Fighter Wing (TFW), the Air Force History Support Division (Pat Engel and Richard Wolf), the Air Force Historical Research Agency (Archie Difante, Tammy Horton, Sly Jackson, and Sam Shearin), and the CAM (Cradle of Aviation Museum) (Joshua Stoff). We are indebted to the photo contributors as credited in the captions, plus the following persons: Jimmy Boyd, Marty Case, George Cully, Bob Delashaw, Bob Dorrough, Joe Gelinger, Tony Gardecki, Frank Hayes, O. C. Hope, Mike Muscat, Howard Plunkett, John Rehm, Gary Retterbush, John Ruffo, Henk Schakelaar, André Wilderdijk, and Larry Van Pelt.

Sources

Histories of the 18th, 36th, 49th, 301st, and 419th TFW, 4520th Combat Crew Training Wing (CCTW), Tactical Air Command (TAC), US Air Forces in Europe (USAFE), Wright Air Development Center (WADC), Air Research and Development Command, Air Proving Ground Center, Air National Guard, and Pacific Air Forces (PACAF).

Published by Key Books
An imprint of Key Publishing Ltd
PO Box 100
Stamford
Lincs PE19 1XQ

www.keypublishing.com

The right of Theo van Geffen and Gerald Arruda to be identified as the authors of this book has been asserted in accordance with the Copyright, Designs and Patents Act 1988 Sections 77 and 78.

Copyright © Theo van Geffen and Gerald Arruda, 2021

ISBN 978 1 913870 66 9

Typeset by SJmagic DESIGN SERVICES, India.

Contents

Chapter 1

1952, the F-105 Takes Shape

Seversky Aircraft Corporation was formed in Farmingdale, Long Island, New York, in 1931 by Soviet emigrant Alexander Seversky. Alexander Kartveli, another Russian emigrant, joined Seversky as Assistant Chief Engineer, later becoming Vice-President and Chief Engineer. In 1939, after a sweeping reorganization, it was decided to change the company's name to Republic Aviation Corporation (RAC). Kartveli was responsible for the design of several military aircraft types, such as the P-47 (15,329 built), the F-84 series (7,524 built), and the F-105. Kartveli considered the F-105 one of the best products RAC ever designed. In 1951–52, Republic was involved in a number of military aircraft development programs. Examples were the XF-84H, YF-84J, F-84X, F-103, the "1957 Fighter-Bomber" and AP-63-FBX (Fighter-Bomber Experimental), which would later become the F-105.

To this author, the coming about of the F-105 is pretty diffuse. Somehow, the F-84X seems to be involved. However, it looks like there was not just one F-84X but two (possibly related) F-84X aircraft. The first one was mentioned by the Air Research and Development Command (ARDC) in its January 1, 1951–December 31, 1952, history. The Command stated, among other things, that although the F-84F was an improvement over the F-84E, with better take-off characteristics and higher maximum speed, there was sentiment in the Air Force that a model improvement of some type in the fighter-bomber field should be planned for the period between the F-84F and a new fighter-bomber. In the fall of 1951, this resulted in the F-84X being placed in the United States Air Force (USAF) program without anything more specific in mind than the obvious fact that the F-84F would not be the best that could be produced in 1954. There was a requirement for a minimum of 401 F-84Xs in a first line fighter-bomber force for a 126 combat wing program. Although no firm configuration for the F-84X had been established, the aircraft production schedule of January 14, 1952, called for the delivery of the first F-84X in March 1954. In late March 1952, ARDC requested the Wright Air Development Center (WADC) to submit a recommendation for the aircraft (or model configuration) to fulfill the F-84X program. This information was necessary for the review of the Fiscal Year 1953 (FY 53) program by the Aircraft and Weapons Board. The second F-84X was a non-funded RAC proposal, initiated in 1951, for an improved and larger F-84F to accommodate an internal weapons bay and ultimately the Pratt & Whitney J57 engine.

In the meantime, the USAF had concluded that it wanted to add a number of features to the Thunderstreak, such as attaching a straight wing spar to replace the "hockey stick" spar, which would simplify fabrication processes considerably, additional electronic and navigation devices and a more complex fire control system. In addition, a still higher thrust engine was to be incorporated, which meant enlarging the air ducts and otherwise re-arranging the fuselage. This all promised to prolong the first line life of the series through 1957 and 1958. However, following an F-84F configuration conference and subsequent considerations of the desirable changes, it became evident that practically every portion of the F-84F would be affected and that this was deemed technically impossible. Based on this, the USAF and RAC decided that rather than update the F-84F, it would be considerably more practical to design a new aircraft. This would not only incorporate the desired changes but would also give it a far greater growth potential.

Kartveli's efforts to develop a "new F-84F" resulted in the AP-63-FBX proposal. With its wing-root inlet ducts, the aircraft bore a remarkable resemblance to the RF-84F Thunderflash. It also featured, among other things, speed brakes, a one-piece, fully maneuverable stabilizer that would provide greater longitudinal stability at faster-than-sound speeds, and auto-pilot. One of the unique features of the proposal, setting it apart from earlier fighter-bombers, was a bomb bay, as previously proposed for the F-84X, which could contain munitions (two 1,000-pound bombs or a single "special" (nuclear) weapon of up to 3,400-pounds) or additional fuel. The engine of choice was the General Electric (GE) J73.

On March 25, 1952, Republic Aviation Corporation (RAC) proposed the AP-63-FBX to the USAF with an Allison J71-A-7 engine vice the GE J73, and with a T-160 gun. Delivery of 160 aircraft was foreseen with the first one in July 1954 and the final 26 in July 1955. Three months later, it had been reviewed by ARDC and Air Materiel Command (AMC). In June, RAC furnished AMC with cost and delivery schedules of a photo reconnaissance version. In the meantime, on May 23, the Air Staff, after the Aircraft and Weapons Board's recommendation, gave the go-ahead decision to develop RAC's AP-63 proposal as successor to the F-84F, rather than an improved F-84F. The new aircraft was designated as the F-105. Of note here is that no General Operational Requirement (GOR) existed at that time for a tactical fighter-bomber weapon system. (That GOR, #49, was finally issued on December 1, 1954. It defined an aircraft having the performance and capabilities of the J75-powered F-105B, in essence making the F-105B an operational requirement.) Also, the F-105 was to be developed under the weapon system concept as WS-306A, with RAC being almost entirely in control, being responsible, for instance, for the integration of the aircraft.

The F-105 was activated as WS-306A on September 10, 1952, when the USAF issued Procurement Directive 53-29 for implementation of the F/RF-105 program. It was worth $13m for pre-production expenses. Fifteen days later, Letter Contract AF 33(600)-22512 was issued, initiating research and development by authorizing RAC only to proceed with procurement of long-lead time contractor-furnished equipment, tooling, tool design, engineering and mockup. The tentative production schedule encompassed 199 aircraft, with the first one to be delivered in January 1955 and the last 40 in June 1956. In November, representatives of the USAF Commands involved in the development, production and operation of the F-105 discussed its configuration aspects. Only tentative agreements were reached as many of the equipment items for the aircraft were still in the development stage.

A total of 833 F-105s were built, two YF-105As, 75 F-105Bs, three JF-105Bs, 610 F-105Ds, and 143 F-105Fs. Of the original 753 D/Fs, 397 (53%) were lost in the air war in Southeast Asia, 334 in combat and 63 operationally. A number of F-105 types were proposed by Republic and ordered by the USAF, but these were subsequently cancelled. They included two-seaters F-105C and F-105E, and reconnaissance versions RF-105B and RF-105D.

Completion by RAC's Experimental Shop of YF-105A 54-0098, the very first Thunderchief, had been planned for July 31, 1955, but fell behind schedule by some 1½ months. The photo shows the aircraft at Republic's Farmingdale, New York, facility shortly after it had left the shop. (via USAF)

On September 18–19, 1955, the first YF-105A (which had been disassembled) was flown by two C-124s to Edwards AFB, California, where it was re-assembled. On October 22, Republic test pilot Rusty Roth made the first flight. YF1 "098" was accepted by the USAF on November 30 and bailed to RAC for Phase I of the test program. (RAC/CAM)

YF-105A 40099 and F-105Bs 40100 and 40101 at Edwards in early 1957. All three aircraft were bailed to Republic. The three aircraft were all flown to Edwards by C-124 Globemasters. (RAC/CAM)

Ship B3 40100 on a test flight near Edwards in the company of an Air Force Flight Test Center F-100D Super Sabre. Its first flight with RAC test pilot Hank Beaird on May 16, 1956, ended in a wheels-up landing, but it could be repaired. (RAC/CAM)

Ship B11 40110 was the next to last F-105 in the original contract to be accepted and delivered, on June 27, 1958. It was also bailed to RAC at Eglin, where it was used for low-level and bombing tests. (RAC/CAM)

On February 16, 1955, a contract change notification re-authorized 15 aircraft for the F-105 program, including, for the first time, three RF-105Bs. Almost two years later, the USAF directed the program's termination, and all three aircraft were reoriented to provide maximum support to the F-105 flight test program and subsequently re-designated as JF-105Bs. At that time, none of the aircraft had been accepted yet. 40105 was to have left RAC's production line as USAF's first RF-105B. The "flattened" nose was typical for the RF-105B. Its first flight was made by Lin Hendrix on July 18, 1957. (RAC/CAM)

This 1958 photo shows two of the RF-105Bs, Ship JF#1B 40105 and JF#2B 40108, in Farmingdale in the company of Ship B8 40106. (RAC/CAM)

F-105D 58-1146, Ship D1, was accepted by and delivered to the USAF on July 31, 1959. Its first flight was made from Farmingdale on June 9, 1959, by RAC test pilot Lin Hendrix. It was lost on September 26, 1960, when the pilot was forced to abort the take-off from Eglin on a Category (Cat) I test flight. He engaged the barrier, resulting in a Class 26 accident. The photo shows "146" and B8 40106, which is about to taxi out for a sortie from Farmingdale. (RAC/CAM)

A colorful F-105D 81155 being towed to the flight line. D10 was accepted on April 22, 1960, and delivered on April 29. Its first nine years were spent at Eglin, initially bailed to Republic and later assigned to the Air Proving Ground Center (APGC). (RAC/CAM)

After two unsuccessful attempts by RAC to procure an F-105 two-seater, the F-105C, and F-105E, the USAF was finally authorized in May 1962 to buy 143 F-105Fs, albeit at the expense of the same number of F-105Ds. After the first flight of F1, F-105F 24412, on June 11, 1963, with Chief Experimental Test Pilot Carl Ardery, it was accepted on June 20 and delivered three days later. It was then flown to Eglin for the flight test program. (RAC/CAM)

Chapter 2

Tactical Air Command in Pictures

In the 1960s, the Tactical Air Forces of the United States Air Force (USAF) consisted of Tactical Air Command (TAC), the United States Air Forces in Europe (USAFE), and Pacific Air Forces (PACAF). When, for instance, a new tactical fighter or transport aircraft was added to USAF's inventory, TAC always had the scoop of introducing the new aircraft. This was also the case with the F-105 Thunderchief.

Initially, the 474th Fighter Bomber Wing (FBW) at Cannon Air Force Base (AFB) was to become the first wing to accept the F-105. This was later changed to the 354th Fighter Day Wing (FDW) at Myrtle Beach, but after the intervention of 9th Air Force, the 4th FDW (on July 1, 1958, the FBW/FBS and FDW/FDS were re-designated as Tactical Fighter Wing/Squadron) at Seymour Johnson would be the first Wing to be equipped with F-105s, initially with three squadrons of Bs and one with Ds, one squadron converting from F-100Cs at a time. The first unit to convert was the 335th FDS, which received its first F-105B on May 27, 1958. However, in the meantime, the 335th "Chiefs" had moved to Eglin AFB to conduct Category (Cat) II/III System Development and Evaluation testing of the F-105B, the first time a new aircraft was tested by the using organization. In this way, the USAF wanted to speed the transition from test to squadron use. The 335th was also the first operational squadron to receive the F-105D with the first two aircraft received on April 15, 1960. To accomplish its Cat II/III testing, the Chiefs transferred Cat III of the F-105B to its sister squadron, the 334th TFS. The first F-105F, 24419, arrived at Nellis AFB, Nevada, on December 7, 1963, joining the 4520th Combat Crew Training Wing (CCTW).

Up to November 8, 1965, TAC had three operational F-105 wings assigned, each with four squadrons: the 4th TFW at Seymour (333rd, 334th, 335th, and 336th TFS), and the 23rd (560th, 561st, 562nd and 563rd TFS) and 355th TFW (354th, 357th, 421st and 469th TFS), both stationed at McConnell. On November 8, not only was the flag of the 355th TFW moved to PACAF's Takhli Royal Thai Air Base (RTAB), but TAC also lost the 333rd, 354th, 357th, 421st and 469th TFS to PACAF in the November 1965–January 1966 period, along with 1,606 personnel and 90 F-105Ds. The 4th and 23rd TFW were then tasked to accomplish replacement pilot training. Combat crew training was accomplished by the 4520th CCTW with initially one CCTS, the 4526th, which was later joined by the 4523rd CCTS. When it became clear the F-105 CCT activities had to be moved from Nellis to make room for F-111A Cat III testing and CCT activities, the 4519th CCTS was activated at McConnell to pick up that task, with resulting movement of personnel and aircraft. Nellis also housed the Fighter Weapons School (FWS) with two major Divisions, the Training Research & Development Division and the Operations and Training Division. By October 10, 1960, its five F-105Ds had been received. On September 1, 1966, the FWS joined the 4525th Fighter Weapons Wing (FWW), which was organized on that date at Nellis. One of its assigned squadrons was the 4537th FWS, which was responsible, among others, for the F-105F Wild Weasel courses. Assigned were F-105Ds and Fs. On October 15, 1969, the 4525th FWW was inactivated and replaced by the 57th FWW. In a similar way, the 4537th FWS became the 66th FWS with no change in mission. On July 15, 1973, the 35th TFW at George AFB, California, already equipped with F-4 Phantoms, became the final Air Force wing with F-105s assigned. In February 1971, TAC's commander, Gen William Momyer, had told the Air Staff that because of problems in achieving an operational capability in the Wild Weasel (WW) F-4C and F-4D aircraft, the F-105F was the only aircraft possessing that capability. His conclusion was that the F-105F had to be retained to fill the void until 1975. Also, that because of the complexity of the WW mission, the aircraft should not be delegated to part-time pilots in the Reserves. Because McConnell was to transfer to Strategic Air Command, a new home had to be found for TAC's F-105F WW squadron, the 561st TFS. Initially, this was to be Eglin, but on July 15, 1973, the Squadron moved from McConnell to George. There, the 561st would form the nucleus of what was to eventually become an anti-surface-to-air missile training center. Long-range plans called for the transfer of the Wild Weasel F-105s to the Reserve Forces in FY 76, provided F-4D WW aircraft would be available as replacements. Three more squadrons at George were equipped with F-105G WW aircraft at one time or another: the 562nd TFS, the 563rd TFTS, and the 39th TFTS.

Right: **F-105B 40111 was the first Thunderchief with a complete fire control system. It was formally delivered to the USAF in Farmingdale on May 27, 1958, when RAC's president Mundy Peale handed the "keys" to Gen O. P. Weyland, TAC's commander. After the ceremony, Lt Col Bob Scott, commander of the 335th TFS, flew the aircraft to Eglin. This November 1958 photo shows SSgt Jim Corriher working in the aft section of "111." (USAF)**

Below: **Project Warn was an Army-Air Force weapons demonstration for President John F. Kennedy at Fort Bragg, North Carolina, in October 1961. One of the participants was F-105B 57-5813 of the 336th TFS that was configured with 26 500-pound bombs for a total of 6.5 tons, a first in a public demonstration. The photo shows "813" at Seymour Johnson prior to its participation. (USAF)**

F-105B 75828 of the 336th TFS became the first Thunderchief to reach 500 flying hours. The February 1962 sortie was flown by Col Albert Evans, 4th TFW commander. In the photo he is congratulating TSgt Duncan McKethan, the aircraft's crew chief. (USAF)

During the Cuban Missile Crisis in October–November 1962, F-105Bs of the 4th TFW were deployed to McCoy AFB, Florida. Some of the aircraft were on air defense alert, like F-105B 75824, which is configured with four AIM-9B Sidewinders. (USAF)

In the period April 1, 1963–January 7, 1964, two of the units of the 4th TFW at Seymour Johnson AFB, the 334th and 336th TFS, accomplished a TDY (Temporary Duty) to Morón AB, Spain, under *Fox Able* to operate their F-105Bs as day fighter interceptors in support of the 65th Air Division, relieving F-104Cs of the 479th TFW (George AFB, California). *Fox Able* was the nickname for deployments of TAC fighter units sent to strengthen the defense of Western Europe. It was the first NATO rotation of F-105s and the first overseas rotation of any F-105 squadron. The photo shows F-104C 60936 of the 436th TFS on the brink of its return to George, with recently arrived F-105B 75815 of the 334th TFS in the background. (USAF)

The 335th TFS was the first operational squadron to convert to the B and D versions of the F-105. Initially, the Ds carried full-color squadron markings as shown on 81153. The aircraft is configured with the Anderson and Greenwood test tow reel and dart target assembly. (RAC/CAM)

The good ol' days when aircraft were still lined up on the flight line and un-camouflaged. The photo shows F-105Ds of the 4th TFW at Seymour Johnson. (USAF)

After the decision to consolidate all F-105 replacement training in the 23rd TFW at McConnell, Kansas, the 4th TFW on November 2, 1966, initiated transfer of its remaining F-105 assets. Its final Thunderchief, D/61-0071, departed Seymour on November 22 (for Nellis). (USAF)

In the October 27–November 12, 1964, period, the 561st TFS participated in Exercise *Goldfire I*. For this purpose, the unit deployed to Naval Air Station (NAS) Olathe, Kansas, with 19 F-105D/Fs and 276 personnel. On the photo is F-105F 63-8343 while on a mission. (USAF)

The 560th TFS of McConnell's 23rd TFW became the first CONUS (Continental United States) unit to support Exercise *Tropic Lightning* in Hawaii by providing close air support (CAS) training to the 25th Infantry Division, which was stationed at Schofield Barracks. The unit deployed to Hickam with six F-105D/Fs, personnel, and equipment in the November 30–December 14, 1964, period. The photo shows F-105D 10133 and F-105F 24433 of the 560th TFS on Hickam's runway prior to take-off. (USAF)

The 561st TFS was one of TAC's F-105D/F squadrons that supported the SIOP (single integrated operational plan) mission of the F-105D/F squadrons at Yokota AB, Japan, which were deployed on TDY to Takhli RTAB, Thailand, to fly combat. The 561st was at Yokota in the March 6–July 10, 1965, period. The photo shows F-105D 24395 while landing at Yokota in May 1965. (Y. Enomoto)

After USAF's July 19, 1967, announcement to also consolidate F-105 combat crew training at McConnell, the 4520th CCTW at Nellis transferred its 16 F-105Bs to the 23rd TFW. Due to the differences between the B and the D, only instructor pilots flew the B models. The photo shows F-105B 75820 of the 563rd TFS, configured with the dart installation. Due to the lack of suitable ranges, each class deployed to George AFB in the final two weeks prior to the graduation to complete its training in, for instance, air combat maneuvering and the AIM-9. (Coll/TvG)

F-105F 38287 of the 4519th CCTS/MG at McConnell in May 1969. (TvG)

In the third quarter of 1970, the replacement training mission of the 23rd TFW at McConnell was further being diminished with the continuing transition to operational status of the 561st, 562nd, and 563rd TFS, and the transfer of the remainder of the RTU mission to the 419th Tactical Fighter Training Squadron (TFTS). The photo shows an F-105F Wild Weasel (561st/MD), an F-105D (562nd/ME), and an F-105D Thunderstick II (563rd/MF). (USAF)

When, on July 1, 1972, the 23rd TFW was moved WOPE (without personnel and equipment) to England AFB, Louisiana, to re-equip with A-7D Corsair IIs, the 561st (Rear), 562nd, and 563rd TFS were reassigned to the 832AD. The last two were inactivated on the 31st (the 419th TFTS was inactivated on October 1, 1971), and the 561st (Rear) became a tenant at McConnell. Rear, because 12 F-105F/Gs, 381 personnel, and equipment had deployed to Korat RTAB in April 1972 as 561st TFS Detachment A and attached to the 388th TFW to enforce US forces in SEA. On July 15, 1973, the PCS (permanent change of station) of the 561st to George was completed and the unit was reassigned to the 35th TFW. In the September 4–14 period, 12 F-105Gs, personnel, and equipment of the Detachment redeployed to George where they joined their parent unit. The photo shows "many fours," F-105G 24444 of Yellow Section (561st TFS), configured with two AGM-45 and one AGM-78 training missiles. (Coll/JA)

F-105G 38292 of Blue Section (562nd TFS) arriving on last chance prior to flying a training sortie. (TvG)

Above: F-105G 38307 of Blue Section taking off from George in the company of a Yellow Section F-105G. (TvG)

Left: F-105G 38303 during in-flight refueling with a KC-135. (Coll/TvG)

After the departure on February 27, 1967, of the final four Thunderchiefs from Europe, it would not be until August 29, 1976, that F-105s returned. On that date, six F-105Gs with 118 personnel and equipment of the 35th TFW flew to Spangdahlem, Germany, in the *Coronet Yankee/Reforger 76* series of short-term deployments from CONUS to Europe, simulating the reinforcement of Europe in times of tension. The unit, known as "Detachment, 561st TFS," was attached to the 52nd TFW and returned to George on September 21. (TvG)

When the first F-4G Advanced Wild Weasel, 90239, arrived at George on April 28, 1978, the 35th TFW had three different WW aircraft assigned, the F-105G, the F-4C, and F-4G. In the photo is F-4G 97205 and F-105G 38345. (TvG)

The 355th TFW was organized at George AFB on July 8, 1962, as TAC's second operational F-105 wing. A little more than two years later, on July 21, the Wing PCS-ed to McConnell to join the 23rd TFW, forming a formidable force of eight squadrons with F-105D/Fs, although, owing to TDY deployments, not all were at McConnell at the same time. The photo shows F-105D 10090 at George. (Howard White)

The 354th TFS was the first unit of the 355th TFW at George to receive the F-105 when three F-105Ds arrived on September 28, 1962. In the January 24–February 12, 1964, period, the squadron participated in two cold weather exercises at Eielson AFB, Alaska, *Diamond Lil XI* and *Polar Siege*. They operated in temperatures ranging from 37°F to minus 43°F. The photo shows a participating flight of four F-105Ds. The third aircraft from the top, 24345, was lost on February 7 owing to flight control problems. The pilot, Capt James Carlson, ejected safely. (USAF)

Most of TAC's operational F-105 squadrons TDY-ed to Japan/Okinawa and/or SEA in 1965 to support the SIOP commitment at Osan, South Korea, or Kadena, Okinawa, and to fly combat from Korat or Takhli RTAB. The 421st TFS was no exception. They deployed, as *Two Buck Three*, from McConnell to support the 18th TFW at Kadena in the April 7–August 27, 1965, period. The photo shows F-105D 59-1823 on its way to Kadena. (Dave Ferguson)

Above: In the month the 388th TFW was organized at McConnell (October 1, 1962), it received 21 F-100C Super Sabres as interim equipage while awaiting the F-100D/Fs from the wings at Itazuke, Japan and Kadena, which would convert to F-105Ds. However, on February 6, 1963, USAF approved TAC's program change proposal to change the 388th TFW program from an F-100D/F to an F-105D/F wing, starting in the fourth quarter of 1963. Until that time, the 560th TFS would essentially be the wing's only aircraft-equipped squadron. The first F-105D arrived at McConnell on November 5, 1963, making the 388th the last of seven operational wings to receive the F-105D. However, the 388th designation would be short-lived, as on February 8, 1964, the 388th was inactivated and replaced by the newly organized 23rd TFW. According to TAC, it was deemed proper to change the numerical designation: the 388th was an older Bomb Group, while the honors of the 23rd Fighter Group more readily identified itself with the mission of the F-105 organization at McConnell. The photo shows bomb load training with F-105D 24401, one of the 21 F-105Ds received by the 388th TFW. (USAF)

Right: On September 21, 1960, the first F-105D, 91718, was formally accepted by TAC at Nellis when BG John Ewbank, commander of the 4520th CCTW, received its "keys" from Mundy Peale, RAC's president. (USAF)

Owing to the fact the 4th TFW was unable to supply enough F-105s for the build-up of the Cuban Missile Crisis force in Florida, the 4520th CCTW was tasked to provide additional F-105Ds. The photo shows two lines of 4520th F-105Ds at McCoy, with the tail of a 335th TFS F-105D on the far right. (USAF)

The 4520th CCTW was responsible for, among other things, F-105D training. This was initially done by one of its squadrons, the 4526th CCTS, but because of the large number of students to be trained, the 4523rd CCTS joined the 4526th on February 5, 1963, when it converted from an F-100 to an F-105 training unit. In the photo, the pilot of F-105D 91750 has extended the speed brakes for his attack on a target on one of the Nellis ranges. (Lucky Ekman)

The addition of F-105 two-seaters to the F-105 curriculum was a big advantage. The first F-105F, 24419, arrived at Nellis on December 7, 1963. The consequence was that each F received "cost" the wing two Ds, for a total of 38 single-seaters. (Lucky Ekman)

Camouflaged F-105D/F aircraft at the Nellis flight line. Note the difference in the tail-number markings. The two Ds in the photo are modified with APR-25/26 RHAW (radar homing and warning) equipment. (USAF)

Although the June 29, 1962, edition of the Nellis base newspaper, *The Century,* had already stated that the Thunderbirds would open their 1963 show season in a new aircraft, the F-105B, it would take until January 29, 1964, before their first aircraft, 75782, was delivered to Nellis. The team flew its first (unofficial) show at Nellis on April 4. The photo shows "782" in the company of F-105D 60-0415 of the 4520th CCTW while on a training sortie near the Grand Canyon. (USAF)

Four Thunderbirds aircraft in formation over typical country in the southwestern part of the US. Note the slot aircraft (75793) with a (blackened) stainless steel vertical stabilizer. (USAF)

The team's seventh show was to be flown at Hamilton AFB, California, on May 10, 1964, with the aircraft arriving the previous day from McChord, Washington, after performing their sixth show. After arriving over Hamilton, the three pilots of the aircraft in the diamond formation (#4, Jerry Shockley, had to abort after take-off and return to McChord) were to pitch up at 5–6 Gs with a four-second interval and land; lead Paul Kauttu first, followed by Gene Devlin and Bill Higginbotham. Kauttu made a standard Thunderbird pitch-up followed by a sharp turning chandelle to a downwind leg of 1,500 feet. Next was Devlin, and as he initiated his pitch-up, his aircraft, 75801, experienced a catastrophic breakup, killing him. The photo shows Devlin's F-105B just after breakup. (via John Lowery)

On September 1, 1966, the 4537th Fighter Weapons Squadron (FWS) was designated and organized at Nellis and assigned to the 4525th Fighter Weapons Wing (FWW). It replaced the F-105 Section of the Fighter Weapons School. The primary mission was to train selected pilot/electronic warfare officer (EWO) aircrews as F-105 Wild Weasel crews. Its OT&E (Operational Test and Evaluation) flight utilized its Combat Tactics Development F-105s to accomplish TAC-directed tests involving F-105 systems and associated armament. The 4537th operated with an average of 14 aircraft possessed to support WW training, four F-105s possessed to support OT&E, and three T-39Bs to support the WW mission. When the USS *Pueblo* was seized by the North Koreans on January 23, 1968, USAF's presence in South Korea was minimal at best. This resulted in an extensive build-up, with units deploying from CONUS as Combat Fox (USAF) and Coronet Wasp (TAC). As all WW F-105Fs were tied up by combat operations in SEA, the 4537th FWS was tasked to send five of its aircraft with aircrews to Osan AB. The aircraft departed on January 28 and arrived on January 31. They stayed assigned to the 4525th FWW but were possessed by the 12th TFS, which had already deployed from Kadena. Aircrews were attached to Whiskey Flight. The photo shows their arrival at Hickam after completing the flight from Nellis. (USAF)

38340 is an F-105F Wild Weasel assigned to the 4537th FWS in May 1969. (TvG)

The 4537th/66th FWS also used the North American T-39B Sabreliner, like 03507 photographed in May 1969. (TvG)

On October 15, 1969, the 66th FWS was activated and assigned to the 57th FWW, absorbing the assets of the 4537th FWS, which was inactivated the same day. The 66th continued the mission of the 4537th. The photo shows two F-105Ds of the 66th FWS, on approach to Nellis. (TvG)

The 66th FWS utilized Wild Weasel F-105Gs until July 25, 1975, when the last Thunderchiefs departed for George to form the nucleus of the 563rd TFTS. F-105G 38328 was one of them and left on July 22, 1975. (TvG)

Chapter 3

The First F-105Ds in Europe

I n 1958, the modernization of US Air Forces in Europe (USAFE) was continued with the introduction of F-100C/D/F Super Sabres, B-66B Destroyers, and F-101A/C and RF-101 Voodoos. Further modernization of its inventory with F-105 Thunderchiefs was in the early planning stage. Spring 1958 F-105 programming scheduled conversion of the 48th TFW to F-105s in the second quarter of 1960 and of the 49th TFW beginning in the third quarter. Both wings were still stationed in France. As it had always been the consequent position of USAFE to convert one

On March 6, 1961, 21 pilots of Class 61J, including ten of Bitburg's 36th TFW, entered the first operational F-105D training course at Nellis AFB, Nevada, as given by the 4526th Combat Crew Training Squadron (CCTS). Upon graduation on May 5, the Bitburg pilots picked up their F-105Ds at Mobile Air Materiel Area (MOAMA) at Brookley for the trip home. The photo shows Col Delashaw, commander of the 36th TFW and student of Class 61J, prior to a training sortie. (USAF)

The crowd at Bitburg was expecting its commander, Col Delashaw, to show up with the very first Thunderchief for USAFE but were surprised to see 1st Lt Retterbush of the 22nd TFS in 00433 instead. The chairs on the viewing platform would be used for the next day's Armed Forces Day. (RAC/CAM)

wing in the UK and the other in Central Europe, on May 20, 1958, USAFE recommended that the USAF change the program to reflect the units as the 36th and 20th TFW, respectively. The proposal would, among other things, phase out the older F-100Cs of the 36th TFW at Bitburg AB (Air Base) in Germany before the newer F-100Ds. Although USAF approved the proposal, its program in mid-1958 still showed the 20th TFW as the first unit to convert, receiving three squadrons with 21 F-105Ds and four F-105Es, commencing in the second quarter of 1960. The 36th would receive its first aircraft that year in the final quarter.

Red Richard

When France refused to grant the US further atomic storage rights, the Supreme Allied Commander Europe/US Commander-in-Chief Europe (SACEUR/USCINCEUR) directed USAFE, in July 1959, to withdraw three nuclear-capable F-100D/F tactical fighter wings from Toul-Rosières AB (50th TFW to Hahn, Germany), Étain (49th TFW to Spangdahlem, Germany), and Chaumont (48th TFW to RAF Lakenheath, UK). The project was called Red Richard. To make the 49th TFW's move possible, the 10th Tactical Reconnaissance Wing at Spangdahlem moved to RAF Alconbury with two squadrons, while one moved to RAF Chelveston and the fourth squadron to RAF Bruntinthorpe. The 49th initiated its move on August 20.

In the meantime, on June 1, 1959, USAFE, based on the latest USAF information, published Programming Plan (PP) 504-59 "F-105 Conversion." One of the objectives was to develop a plan for an orderly conversion of the 36th, 20th, and 49th TFW to 75 F-105Ds, in a manner that would assure a minimum loss in combat capability and ensure maximum flying safety. Tactical Air Command (TAC) was to accomplish initial aircrew training for both conversion and pipeline pilots. Pilot selection would initially be based on utilizing previously qualified Century-series aircraft bomb commanders whose assignments would be 1½ or more years in theater after completing the conversion training. First, pilots would be fed into the Nellis training program at a rate of ten per month, beginning in the first quarter of 1961. The latest changes and unit equipping schedules were then incorporated in a revised PP 504-59. The 22nd TFS was to start converting in the second quarter of 1961, the 55th TFS (20th TFW) in the first quarter of 1962, and the 7th TFS (49th TFW) in the third quarter of 1962. USAFE's request for a total of 222 F-105D trained pilots was granted by the end of 1960.

Revision

USAF Program Guidance 62-1 reduced USAFE's F-105 conversion from nine squadrons to six, eliminating the 20th TFW, and increased the number of PACAF squadrons from three to six. This resulted in a series of messages between USAF and USAFE. For instance, on February 10, 1960, USAFE emphasized that this reduction would jeopardize its combat capability and urgently requested reinstatement of the three squadrons. On February 25, USAF informed USAFE that programming documents were being amended, reflecting that the 36th TFW was to begin conversion in the first quarter of 1961 and the 49th in the fourth quarter. If conversion of a third wing could be materialized, it would be the 48th TFW, as USAFE had requested. In addition, the GAM-83 Bullpup was a requirement with the F-105D. This information forced USAFE to publish an almost complete revision of PP 504-59. It also resulted in numerous projects that were in progress, or nearing completion, having to be relocated or even abandoned. It was published on May 18. Some three months later, USAFE was informed that

Some three weeks after arriving at Bitburg, two F-105Ds, 00436 and 00452, both from the 22nd TFS, participated in the Paris Air Show. One was on static display and the other one was flying, although this was alternated. During a June 9 ceremony there, Gen Smith, USAFE commander, officially accepted the first F-105D (00436) for his command. (W. Gysin)

1st Lt Retterbush and Capt Wyrick were selected to accompany the two F-105Ds to Paris. On the photo, they are being introduced to Mundy Peale, the President of the Republic Aviation Corporation. (via Gary Retterbush)

an extensive review of overall USAF operational requirements for modernization of tactical forces was completed. USAFE was told that in view of earlier discussions, no change in its F-105D conversion program was contemplated.

In a September 17, 1960, message to 17th Air Force (17AF) "F-105D Conversion Program," USAFE stated that, based on a firm USAF F-105D delivery schedule through December 1961, a projected delivery schedule through April 1962, and TAC's projected class entry/graduation dates for F-105D Course 111506E at Nellis, a detailed conversion plan was established and submitted as the basis for planning by all concerned. Also, that PP 504-59 would be amended to include the plan as a firm objective. The first unit to convert would be the 22nd TFS, which would stand down on January 1, 1961.

Vigorously

In a personal letter dated September 22, 1960, to USAFE's commander, Gen Frederic Smith, TAC's vice commander, Gen Jacob Smart, stated that TAC had evaluated the F-105D weapon system and had found that the aircraft would not be ready for deployment unless USAFE was willing to accept an extremely low operational readiness (OR) rate for a considerable period of time. Gen Smart told Gen Smith that TAC's experience with the F-105B, which was a considerably less sophisticated weapon system, indicated unsatisfactory support and that a large number of modifications on the D model would be necessary during the next 12 months. Gen Smith reacted on October 15, stating he shared the concern about the aircraft's OR problems. Nonetheless, for many reasons, USAFE vigorously resisted any slippages in the D's deployment unless they could not be operated at all. Even without a completely effective F-105D radar capability during the early stages of the conversion, it was felt that the aircraft's capability would far exceed that of the F-100C/Mk-7 weapon system.

Officially

On October 12, 1960, Project AFE 0F-477 was established for delivery of F-105Ds to Bitburg. Completion was scheduled for September 1961. The planning of the *High Flight* movement to Europe was the responsibility of the 4440th Aircraft Delivery Group (ADG) with headquarters at Langley AFB, Virginia. The Group had worldwide detachments with, for instance, Det 6 at Chateauroux AB in France.

After it became clear that the 36th TFW would be the first USAFE wing to convert, the Wing initiated preliminary planning shortly before June 30, 1960. In August, Mobile Training Detachment (MTD) 740A (F-105-3) was assigned to Bitburg. Floor plans were submitted and approved for the adaptation of three buildings to the MTD. By the year's end, the MTD was firmly in place. On January 3, 1961, class instructions in all phases of the school program began, with 75 students entering 12 classes. Although the program progressed satisfactorily overall, the lack of test equipment hampered complete indoctrination in some of the courses. Based on the complexity of the F-105D compared to the F-100C, an increase of 425 maintenance spaces was approved. To support the Bitburg program, requirements for Contract Technical Representatives were established. Justification narratives and job descriptions were then sent to 17AF for approval.

In November, a MOAMA/RAC Supply and Facility Assistance Team visited to assist with the overall problems of the F-105 conversion. Among other things, the team briefed personnel and surveyed storage capability and facilities to be used in support of the F-105 weapon system. The team's conclusion was that Bitburg was prepared to receive the new aircraft, supplies, and storage materiel. New and refurbished maintenance facilities included, for example, a permanent 12,100sq ft armament and electronics facility, a J-75 engine trim pad, and a building for the instrument shop.

The first of the F-105Ds for the 49th TFW arrived at Spangdahlem on October 30, 1961. It was 10041 and flown by the Wing commander, Col Wilbur Grumbles. At MOAMA, its nose was adorned with a map of Texas with a white star and the name *Kordel-Eden*. It was in honor of the sister-city status of his hometown, Eden, in Texas and Kordel, a small town near Spangdahlem. (USAF)

The first F-105F two-seater for the 36th TFW and USAFE, 24424, arrived on February 20, 1964. It was flown from MOAMA to Bitburg by RAC test pilot Harry Evans with BG R. Allison, USAFE's Assistant Deputy for Operations, in the rear seat; 24432 arrived as well. (Coll/TvG)

Gen Smith officially announced on January 30, 1961, that the 36th TFW would convert to the F-105D. Nine days later, 36th TFW officials announced that the 22nd TFS "Bumblebees" was the first of the Wing's squadrons to convert and that the first group of pilots would leave shortly for training at Nellis.

In the meantime, the Squadron was relieved of all operational commitments: the Victor Alert commitment, involving four F-100C aircraft, was discontinued (and was not reassigned to another organization), and its automatic strike commitments were redistributed to other 17AF organizations other than the 36th TFW. As of January 18, the 22nd conducted requalification of in-flight refueling. Each of the 23 pilots flew three sorties, accomplishing three rendezvous with an average of 27 "dry" and six "wet" hook-ups. The first five F-100Cs were transferred to the Air National Guard (ANG) on January 30, while the final Squadron aircraft left on June 18. To prepare the pilots for their transition training, a Nellis instructor team arrived at Bitburg in late January to conduct a two-week introductory course, including, among other things, the basic electronics, the AN/APN-105 Doppler navigator, and the R-14 radar. This was followed in mid-February by a two-week course on the basic F-105D systems by the MTD. The first class went off to Nellis in late February and started training on March 6, 1961. The 22nd had pilots in three different classes. A class started every 30 days with each class lasting 60 days. Upon graduation, the pilots proceeded to MOAMA at Brookley AFB, Alabama, to pick up an F-105D for ferrying to Bitburg. MOAMA had prepared the F-105Ds, which had been flown to Brookley from RAC's facility at Farmingdale after their acceptance by the Air Force. The pilots flew an acceptance and KB-50J refueling sortie in the aircraft released by MOAMA. By late April, delivery of the first F-105D increment to the 22nd TFS was scheduled for May 11–12. Ferry would take place through in-flight refueling. However, in the meantime, it was reported that in-flight refueling testing with the F-105D at Wright-Patterson AFB, Ohio, was carried out with problems. When they could not be resolved in time, delivery would be made by "island hopping": Brookley–Seymour Johnson–Harmon–Lajes–Chateauroux–Bitburg.

Commander

On May 12, Det 10 of the 4440th ADG at Brookley launched the initial flight of four F-105Ds for a non-stop flight to Bitburg. It was no surprise that Col Bob Delashaw, 36th TFW commander, was one of the four pilots. He assumed command of the wing on July 18, 1960, after serving as USAFE's Deputy Director for Requirements. There he developed plans and requirements for the F-105. Col Delashaw flew 64 P-47 combat sorties in Europe. The Colonel stated, "With most pilots having considerable experience in subsonic aircraft, there were not many problems in transitioning into the F-105D. What differed was the fact they had to learn the use of the instruments and all the attributes the D had. It took a while to get through with a lot of study." The other pilots were Capt Roger Nelson of the 23rd TFS, flying Delashaw's Wing as "2," Capt Dalton "Mac" McCullar as "3" in 00451, with 1st Lt Gary Retterbush flying McCullar's Wing as "4" in 00433 (both of the 22nd). Delashaw's aircraft, 00436, had been painted in the red/blue/yellow wing colors, while the tails of the other three aircraft adorned the three red stripes of the Bumblebees.

(On March 8, 1962, the maintenance functions and aircraft were transferred from the fighter squadrons to the newly activated 36th Consolidated Aircraft Maintenance Squadron. It became the largest squadron at Bitburg, with about 1,400 authorized spaces. Maintenance was divided into three flights: "Red" for the 22nd, "Blue" for the 23rd, and "Yellow" for the 53rd, with individual colors being retained. However, after an inspection on March 25 by 17AF and USAFE, this distinction was also lost when the Wing was directed to completely implement Air Force Manual (AFM) 66-1 for wing maintenance. By many, this was called "communist maintenance." From then on, colored triangles, denoting the flights, were carried under the left cockpit rail.

Col Delashaw commented, "After having gotten out on top after take-off, I just did not feel good with the autopilot. However, when we went to the first refueling off of Jacksonville (Florida), it

F-105Ds 00430 and 00469, and F-105F 38304 of Blue Flight (23rd TFS) on the flight line at Wheelus in March 1965. On April 5, 1965, "469" became the first USAFE F-105 with 1,000 flying hours. The pilot was Lt Col Robert White, the commander of the 36th TFW training detachment at Wheelus, while the crew chiefs were A1C Joel Davis and A2C John Walker. RAC's technical representative, Bill Stuart, presented a 20-inch F-105 model to Lt Col White, who gave it to Davis. (Al Mikutis)

From the F-105D/F the 36th TFW converted to the F-4D. The first Phantom II, 40933, arrived at Bitburg on March 20, 1966. The aircraft was escorted by two F-105s. By June 30, the Wing had 46 F-4Ds. (USAF)

went smoothly. At the ocean station ship *ECHO*, we had our second KB-50J 'encounter' without a problem." He took over the lead, and when the four aircraft approached the Azores, they were refueled again. He got on the left drogue of the left KB-50J and received, according to procedures, 500 pounds of fuel. He continued:

> I was watching my instruments, which indicated that my speed was decreasing. I was hollering and fussing at them but started to let down to pick up more speed. But it kept going down while trying to hang on to that drogue. This bothered me a little. We went into a cloud at that time and the airspeed just went to zero. It was not just the tape instrument, but also the standby system. This really concerned me.

When Delashaw came off the drogue, he dropped the nose to pick up some speed. When he was on the verge of going into Mach 1, he pulled the throttle back a little. When he looked in front of him, Delashaw saw the contrails of the other three aircraft. He explained:

> I called and told them I would be joining them. I did and discussed with McCullar what to do. We decided I could make it to Spain versus Chateauroux where we would have our final refueling. Nelson would join me to Torrejón AB [Spain]. I did not have a map of the base and did not know how long the runway was.

The two landed and spent the night at Torrejón. Although Delashaw had not planned on using the drag chute, he supposedly pulled the handle. However, it had not fully deployed, but popped out of its container, meaning he could not take off nor land with it. In addition, he had hit a rough spot while landing, resulting in a tire change. Delashaw recalled:

I called Bitburg and they said they would send down RAC Tech Reps and maintenance and take charge. I never understood why the speed went to zero. The indicator was still sitting at zero. It looked like I did not have the pitot meter on. I just stayed overnight and the next day they sent an F-100F to pick me up as we would have our Armed Forces Day that Saturday.

As Capt Nelson had not used his drag chute, he returned to Bitburg before the F-100F returned with Delashaw. His aircraft then received a new wheel and tire, and the pitot system was treated with nitrogen and dried out, as they were fairly sure this was the problem. They later flew Retterbush in, and he flew "436" to Bitburg on the 16th. It meant Col Delashaw was not the pilot who landed the very first F-105D Thunderchief at Bitburg as was scheduled, but 1st Lt Gary Retterbush.

By the book

There was a big difference between flying the F-100C and the F-105D, according to Retterbush: "Go low, far, fast and carry a big stick." With regard to the final part of the ferry flight he stated:

When Delashaw and Nelson were forced to divert to Spain, lead could certainly have said we all go to Spain, but Mac and I were already off the tanker and on our way and Delashaw was too big of a man to recall us so he could be first. By the way, the commander never let me jokingly forget I "stole" this opportunity. Of course, all of the big brass in Europe was at Bitburg to welcome me, but a first lieutenant was all they got.

On June 21, 1966, Bitburg lost its final two Thunderchiefs when 00465 and 00493 departed for MOAMA at Brookley for major overhaul. This photo shows "465" taxiing at Bitburg with the blue stripes of the 23rd TFS. (USAF)

The final loss of a USAFE F-105 took place on July 14, 1966, when F-105F 38310 of Spangdahlem's 7th TFS was lost on a low-level radar navigation mission in company of an F-105D. Both crew members were also lost. "310" is at the Wheelus flight line with a MN-1A weapon dispenser on the centerline pylon. (via André Wilderdijk)

There was more to this, according to Retterbush:

At that time, the F-105 had a problem with the refueling manifold pipeline and we were not supposed to really top off when refueling. When I had found my tanker at the Azores, I "forgot" about topping off and got a full load. Mac did it by the book, got less and thus had to get an additional refueling over France, allowing me to land at Bitburg first after a 4,550-mile, 9½-hour flight. Mac landed about 20 minutes later.

They were met outside Bitburg by an F-100 piloted by Maj Stanley Evers, the 22nd TFS Operations Officer. Conversion to the F-105D also meant it was the fourth time the 36th had been the first wing in Europe to introduce a new jet aircraft (F-80, F-100, and F-102). After the arrival, the two aircraft were placed on display for the joint Bitburg–Spangdahlem Armed Forces Day celebration.

Final

After the arrival of the first aircraft, Operations started making plans for the policies that were necessary for the local operation of a new airplane and the training necessary to bring the unit back on combat-ready status. Col Delashaw said:

Shortly after arriving at "Bit," we started a program of low-level radar navigation training missions in Western Europe, often to the Suippes range in France. We limited those missions to 500 feet with always two aircraft, one pilot "under the hood," flying instruments and watching the radar, and the other one for safety. We spent a lot of time doing this. The R-14 radar at that time took a lot of imagination to discern where you were and what was going by you.

As of May 31, the 22nd TFS had received 16 of its 25 F-105Ds. Of the 25 aircraft, only five did not make it all the way on the first flight. Besides, Col Delashaw and his wingman, Capt Richard Dutton, had to land in Bermuda on June 9, as he could not get his external tanks to take fuel. Dutton's wingman landed as well. Six days later, Capt Rod Giffin returned to Brookley after take-off, as he was unable to get his external tanks to feed. On June 26, Giffin ferried the 25th, and final, F-105D for the 22nd to Bitburg. As programmed, the Bumblebees achieved OR on September 8 and assumed the Victor Alert commitment with four Thunderchiefs.

Epilogue

The Thunderchief made its public debut in June at the 1961 Paris International Air Show at Le Bourget, where during a June 9 ceremony, Gen Frederic Smith, USAFE commander, officially accepted the first F-105D (00436) under his command. The 36th TFW sent a second aircraft (one for static display and one flying). They were switched once. Capt Doyal Wyrick of the 23rd TFS, 1st Lt Retterbush, and a few maintenance troops were chosen to represent the Wing. Retterbush stated:

> We encountered no problems. It was one of the best TDYs [temporary duties] I ever had. Getting paid extra to show off, a fighter pilot's dream! There was no restriction on flying the 105 at Paris other than trying not to go supersonic. The flight was rather short, probably about fifteen minutes. We had a bet with the Navy troops who had the F-4 there that we could get the 105 airborne with less runway than the "Double Ugly." We trimmed the engine to absolute max, used water injection and put on just enough fuel for the show, plus five minutes. We did in fact get off earlier by about 150 feet!

On December 15, 1961, Retterbush had to eject while on an F-105D (60-5383) ferry flight from Bitburg to Spangdahlem, a distance you could easily walk! While he was at altitude, the engine flamed out. Although he was able to restart it, the aircraft would not accelerate and flamed out again. Although not recommended, he decided to dead stick "383" in at Cologne Bonn Airport. While on short finals, the controls froze. Retterbush ejected and was picked up by a chopper. He had "only" twisted his back a little.

USAFE's final four F-105s, all Ds, left the 49th TFW and Spangdahlem on February 24, 1967. Via Torrejón, Spain, the aircraft were flown to Seymour Johnson in the US. F-105D 10106 of the 9th TFS was one of the four Thunderchiefs. The Wheelus photo shows 10106 being prepared for a next mission to the El Uotia Range. (via André Wilderdijk)

While on assignment as an F-105D instructor at Nellis, Retterbush volunteered to fly combat in Southeast Asia (SEA) and was assigned to the 357th TFS at Takhli Royal Thai Air Base, which flew F-105D/Fs. In September 1966, he returned to Germany where he was assigned to the 7th TFS at Spangdahlem. The 49th TFW was preparing to convert from F-105D/Fs to F-4D Phantoms. On February 24, 1967, the last four USAFE F-105Ds departed "Spang" for Seymour Johnson, North Carolina. Retterbush was lead with the other pilots being Capts Robert Jackson, Dick Arnold, and Robert Dorrough, all of the 7th TFS. Retterbush stated:

> Although I was lead, I took off last. I certainly recall the horrible weather on that day. It was actually a bit below minimums when we finally took off. The weatherman closed his eyes for a couple of minutes and stretched the truth so we could depart. I had promised the wing commander a flyby before we departed, and we did one. The Thunderbirds would have been envious of us that day! Our four-ship formation was so low and so tight that even those who saw us pop out of the clouds could not believe it! I remember the wingman who was on the bottom during the final turn to the runway, which we could not see, politely telling me, "Lead, don't forget I'm down here."

This made Retterbush the pilot who not only flew in the very first F-105D for USAFE but also the one who flew out its final F-105D. Retterbush continued, "I had a lot of fun in the Thunderchief and still say it was one of the finest airplanes ever built. I loved her and always will!" The Thuds first flew to Torrejón where a maintenance contingent of the 7th TFS awaited, getting them airborne the next Monday. The first aerial refueling took place shortly after passing Portugal and the final one after passing Bermuda. He returned to Spang after completing F-4 school at Davis-Monthan AFB.

Retterbush collected a total of 1,356 flying hours in the Thunderchief. Of course, there was some friendly animosity between F-105D and F-4 drivers. "We used to joke that we would trade the F-4's back seater for 500 pounds of gas any day," said Retterbush. He continued, "Same for the engines, trade one P&W for two GE ones."

Yet, despite his love for the Thunderchief, Retterbush, assigned to the 35th TFS at Kunsan, South Korea, but on temporary assignment to the 388th TFW at Korat RTAB, downed a North Vietnamese MiG-21 on September 12 and one on October 8, 1972, while using the gun of his F-4E. And on both occasions, his Phantom did have a back seater (1st Lt Dan Autrey and Capt Bob Jasperson, respectively) and two GE engines!

F-105D 10093 has just landed at Wheelus from Spangdahlem in the ferry configuration. The red color on the front wheel door tells us that "093" is a 9th TFS aircraft. (via André Wilderdijk)

Chapter 4

US Air Forces in Europe in Pictures

F-105D 00461 of the 23rd TFS (blue) over the Atlantic, while on a *High Flight* delivery from Brookley to Bitburg on July 20, 1961. The aircraft is about to be refueled by a KB-50J tanker. (Norm Powell)

Wheelus AB was the only USAFE air base, having ranges in the European theater for gunnery, bombing, and missile practice. The USAFE Weapons Center was responsible, with Wheelus being operated by the 7272nd Air Base Wing. USAFE's all-weather interceptor and tactical fighter detachments deployed to Wheelus on a pre-planned basis to accomplish their yearly weapons training. (Col Anderson)

Above: The J-75 engine of F-105D 00527 of the 53rd TFS (yellow stripes) is cartridge-started by the pilot at Wheelus for a training sortie at the El Uotia Range. (Norm Powell)

Left: A crew chief is re-installing the drag chute of an F-105D of the 36th TFW while deployed to Wheelus AB. (Harry Hennigar)

Not everything always goes the right way. On October 2, 1962, Maj Joseph Lamont of the 22nd TFS blew both main tires of F-105D 00522 on landing at Bitburg. When he left the runway, the right main gear collapsed. On November 16, a new left wing arrived and was installed three days later. (John Lowery)

Above: F-105Ds 05374 and 00443 on the flight line; "374" is assigned to Blue Flight (22nd TFS). Note the difference in tail markings. (Jim Arthur)

Right: Squadron exchanges between NATO fighter squadrons in the 1960s were quite common. In the March 31–April 11, 1965, period, the 23rd TFS visited Cambrai AB in France with six F-105D/Fs, while 2/12 Escadron visited Bitburg with six Super Mystère F2s. (USAF)

Below: F-105D 10070 was supposedly the first USAFE camouflaged F-105 and as such shown on the May 1965 Armed Forces Day at Spangdahlem. 00478 was another camouflaged example and is shown here during the ferry flight from Europe to CONUS on March 19, 1966. (Bill Palmer)

Big Lift was a JCS-sponsored, unscheduled strategic mobility exercise and rapid deployment demonstration of America's capability to airlift forces to reinforce NATO rapidly. It took place October 19–December 4, 1963. CONUS fighter forces included 18 F-105Ds and F-104Cs, and 62 F-100D/Fs. USAFE units also participated, and the photo shows three 49th TFW F-105Ds while on a mission against the 2nd Armored Division. (USAF)

After the 7th TFS had hosted 16 Squadron with Canberra B(I)8s at Spangdahlem in July 1964, 16 Squadron returned the favor in August while hosting four F-105Ds at RAF Laarbruch. The photo was made over Laarbruch with an F95, 4-inch lens port oblique camera of a second Canberra. (Graham Pitchfork)

F-105F 38326 of the 49th TFW as seen in December 1965, from a KC-135 Stratotanker during a refueling mission. (Richard Kierbow)

TAC's 4440th ADG at Langley was responsible for the worldwide ferry of USAF aircraft. For this purpose, it loaned pilots. The *High Flight* of F-105D/Fs returning to CONUS was initiated at Torrejón. On the photo, four F-105D pilots are being dropped off to pre-flight their aircraft. Note that only one pilot is wearing his G-suit. (USAF)

Chapter 5

William Tell, 1962

The 3595th Pilot Training Wing (Advanced Single Engine) at Las Vegas AFB, Nevada, which became Nellis on May 1, 1950, initiated a contest, the United States Air Force Gunnery Meet, in the May 2–12, 1949, period, with three-person teams representing 14 units from around the Air Force. They flew two classes of aircraft; the conventional class included F-47s, F-51s, and F-82s, while the jet fighter class included F-80s and F-84s. The winning team was from the 332nd Fighter Group, "Tuskegee Airmen," flying P-47N Thunderbolts. The legacy of William Tell began in June 1954 as the USAF Fighter Gunnery and Weapons Meet III. It was the first all-jet meet and consisted of day fighter and air-to-air rocketry phases. The former was hosted by Nellis, with eight teams participating, including ones from Europe and the Far East. The latter was hosted by Vincent AFB, Arizona, with four "home" teams participating, flying F-86Ds and F-94Cs. Meets were held in 1955 and 1956, but 1957 was skipped.

1958
On October 13, 1958, the USAF Worldwide Fighter Weapons Meet began, the first Meet known by the nickname "William Tell" (WT). As before, there were two phases: the tactical phase at Indian Springs

The overall winner (reciprocating type aircraft) in the first USAF Gunnery Meet at Las Vegas AFB on May 2, 1949, was the 332nd Fighter Group (Tuskegee Airmen) with P-47N Thunderbolts. The primary team members were Capt Alva Temple (L, 301st FS), 1st Lts Harry Stewart (M, 100th FS) and James Harvey (R, 99th FS). Missing from the photo is 1st Lt Halbert Alexander (99th FS). (USAF)

AFB, Nevada, and the air-to-air phase at, for the first time, Tyndall, Florida. It was the last year that both phases took place concurrently: the tactical phase was to take place in even years and the air-to-air phase in odd years.

The 4th TFW at Seymour Johnson was involved in William Tell 1958 with two different types of aircraft, the F-100C Super Sabre in the competition and the F-105B Thunderchief. The 335th TFS, the first Air Force unit to receive the F-105B, deployed some of its aircraft to Nellis to perform flybys for visiting dignitaries, while aircraft were also on static display.

1960

The first of several planning conferences for the 1960 Weapons Meet was held October 5–9, 1959, at the Pentagon. During this conference, the dates, location, and concept of operations were established. The rules were then written by a rules committee at Nellis and published on April 22, 1960. Rule 3.a.(2) stated, "Enter a minimum of one team to compete in all sorties in both high-explosive and nuclear events. Maximum participation will be as follows: 1 F-105 Team, 1 F-104 Team, 1 F-100 Team (Tactical Units), 1 F-100 Team (Training Complex)."

In the meantime, in a November 6, 1959, letter to TAC, USAF mentioned the possible participation of the F-105B in WT 1960. This letter also reached Col Roland McCoskrie, the Director of Training for 9AF at Shaw AFB, South Carolina. In a December 17 letter to 9AF's Deputy of Operations, McCoskrie

Training for William Tell 1962 for both the 36th and 49th TFWs took place at Wheelus AB in Libya. The photo shows the maintenance team for the 36th with Capt Rod Giffin, the team's operations and maintenance officer. (John Ruffo)

stated that with the Meet being scheduled in October 1960, it would require maximum support to commence not later than late July. Experience had proven that it would take a minimum of one squadron of aircraft and pilots plus full wing supply support and the best maintenance personnel. He believed the participation of an F-105 weapons team in 1960 would be beyond the adequate support capability of the 4th TFW in view of other overriding commitments like rotations to Aviano AB, Italy, conversions, training, and testing.

Despite the Colonel's reservations, F-105 participation was still anticipated in the early planning. However, it was also observed that certain restrictions as to armament and nuclear weapons participation would have to be applied, even at the sacrifice of realism. Furthermore, on May 19, all F-105s were grounded because of a locking condition that resulted from freezing of the roll trim actuator. Aircraft were ungrounded four days later but were restricted to flight below freezing level, which was around 13,000 feet. Indecision as to the William Tell project continued, but on May 27, TAC indicated a decision would be forthcoming by July 1. In early June, the 4th TFW indicated it would like to participate, which then could be part of its Cat III testing of the F-105B. In a June 13 message to 9AF, TAC stated that it agreed and directed the 4th TFW to prepare F-105Bs for participation. Three days later, TAC sent out a message, which included the following information, "TAC F-105 team will participate." However, within a few days, this position began to change. On June 22, 12AF informed

Weapons loaders of the 4th TFW busy configuring one of their aircraft with a GAM-83 Bullpup, five of which were expended during the Meet. (USAF)

10144 was one of the three brand-new F-105Ds the 4th TFW picked up at Republic in Farmingdale to participate in WT 62. Here "144" is being loaded with a "shape" in its bomb bay. (USAF)

TAC and 9AF that, owing to additional factors concerning aircraft capabilities and support available, it was apparently premature to consider the F-105B operationally capable to compete. Five days later, 9AF received a message in which TAC rescinded its earlier messages on the Thunderchief's participation and notified the 4th TFW that its first priority was reaching combat readiness (CR), an important part of Cat III testing. However, TAC left the door ajar: participation would be permitted only if it in no way interfered with F-105B Cat III testing or otherwise delayed reaching the CR status. Despite an early July 9AF and 4th TFW message to TAC, stating a decision had been made not to let the F-105Bs participate, TAC still considered this a tentative decision. Finally, on July 29, TAC made it official that the 4th would not participate due to aircraft being in a modification program, Project Optimize, and the possibility of conflicting with Cat III testing.

William Tell 1960 took place on October 3–10 with one F-104C and four F-100D units. Although no F-105Bs participated, one of the highlights was their participation in the fire power demonstration on October 11, during which two F-105Bs of the 334th TFS performed a sonic boom. The Squadron had deployed to Nellis on October 1 with ten pilots and ten F-105Bs. A total of 134 hours were flown, and the in-commission rate was 100%.

1962

Following the 1960 Meet, a William Tell 1962 conference was held at the Pentagon on October 10–13 to make tentative plans for a meet at Nellis for late September or October 1962. The PACAF representative stated that the Command did not plan to enter an F-105D team because of the planned

F-100/F-105 conversions at Itazuke and Kadena ABs (in Japan and Okinawa, respectively). It was also doubtful that an F-100D team could be entered for the same reason and because of the SIOP target coverage program.

On May 3, 1962, the Department of the Air Force published OPlan (Operations Plan) 6-62, "USAF Tactical Fighter Weapons Meet William Tell 1962." Initially, only F-100D squadrons were to participate, but finally, after months of indecision, tactical wings worldwide were directed to enter a team, including F-104C and F-105D wings.

The Meet was sponsored and directed by USAF through its Operations Order (OPORD) 27-62 and hosted by the 4520th CCTW at Nellis. Realism was the keynote, and the order of the day was, "Make it tough and realistic." The competition was designed as a rugged test of combat proficiency, approaching, as closely as possible, actual battlefield conditions. There would be several "firsts": (1) the traditional team concept was scrapped in favor of a single pilot representing his wing (he would have an alternate); (2) the firing of the GAM-83 Bullpup; (3) inclusion of a reconnaissance competition among crews of PACAF, TAC, and USAFE, flying RF-101C Voodoos; (4) CCTWs were excluded; and (5) the testing of the full array of the tactical weapons system, which would bring in aircraft that had an all-weather capability and the use of its integrated bombing and radar system, read the F-105D.

In addition to the 4520th CCTW, the F-105D schoolhouse, the USAF had three full combat wings with F-105Ds; the 4th TFW, 36th and 49th TFWs. In the meantime, TAC's commander Gen Walter Sweeney

Two 49th TFW F-105Ds on the brink of another WT 62 mission. Each aircraft is configured with two M-117 750-pound bombs. The nose is of an F-100D of the 48th TFW of RAF Lakenheath. (USAF)

10154 of the 49th TFW is configured with one M-117 on each outboard pylon on its way to the runway. (USAF)

had grounded, as of June 20, the entire TAC F-105 fleet, resulting in the establishment of a major two-phase worldwide F-105 modification program, Look-Alike, by the USAF in July. It proved that this situation would affect all three participants. In order to enable the 4th TFW to participate, they had to pick up brand-new Block 20RE F-105Ds and fly them to Nellis. On August 29, the three were the only OR F-105Ds the wing possessed! In addition, prior to and during the competition, hangar space at Nellis – used, for instance, to peak up the weapon systems for their new F-105Ds – was a problem, as all the space was saturated with F-105s going through the first phase of Look-Alike. The Thunderchiefs also required precision power supply, and this was only available in F-105 hangars.

4th TFW

On August 6, Capt Tony Gardecki and 1st Lt Jim Craig of the 335th TFS at Seymour Johnson deployed to Nellis with project officer Lt Col Paul Hoza (the Squadron commander) and 14–15 experienced maintenance personnel for pre-meet practice. Capt Gardecki said:

> We picked up three F-105Ds at Farmingdale and flew them to Nellis. TAC gave special clearance for this. At Nellis we had several weeks of training. There they were joined by ten personnel of the Armament Branch of the 4th Armament and Electronic Maintenance Squadron. It also included a competition to determine who would become the primary pilot to carry the colors of the 4th TFW. In my opinion we were selected by Hoza based on our gunnery records. I ended up as the primary pilot.

According to Capt Gardecki, the pace at William Tell was rather demanding. The targets for the next day were received very late in the afternoon. Then all the planning had to be done, and the next day it was getting up early to fly the mission. In addition to the 12 events all tactical fighter participants had to fly, the three Thunderchief pilots flew two sorties in a special radar/navigation bombing competition, utilizing the R-14 radar and APN-131 Doppler. The John L. Mitchell Trophy would be for the winner. Only the F-105Ds had all-weather radar bombing capability.

As Gardecki stated:

The two 55-minute sorties, covering 400 miles each, were hooded low-altitude (between 2,000 and 3,000 feet) toss-bombing missions, Blind Target Identification Point and Blind Identification Point. Immediately after take-off, the pilot went under the hood, a pull-over canvas cover over the canopy cutting off all visual reference to the ground. The sorties included navigation to the target, arrival within a limited time span, spending a minimum amount of time in that area, delivery of a simulated nuclear weapon while the pilot executed a half-loop (impact had to occur within one minute of the pre-calculated time), performing a half-roll to escape the blast, and navigation to Nellis. The chase aircraft made a radio check every five minutes. The F-105D's configuration was two 450-gallon fuel tanks and a BDU-3B installed in the bomb bay. The "target" was of a radar reflector type, which precluded a visual delivery maneuvering.

Out of the 6,000 possible points, Capt Gardecki collected 3,418, Muskat 3,156, and Ruffo 2,659, meaning Gardecki had won the John L. Mitchell Trophy. "A beautiful trophy with a lot of famous names engraved," according to Gardecki. He stated that there was no animosity among his F-105D colleagues.

F-105D 10160 of Team Spangdahlem in flight on the Nellis range. (USAF)

Both "English" F-100 Super Sabre wings also participated in WT 62. F-100Ds 63236 and 63321 belong to the 48th and 62974 and 63001 to the 20th TFW. The first tail is of a TAC F-84F. (USAF)

The three Seymour Johnson aircraft flew a grand total of 142 sorties during the 1½-month of pre-meet practice and the Meet itself, collecting 180 flying hours. Expended were five GAM-83As, 11,719 20-mm cartridges, 434 bombs, and 253 rockets. Upon completion of the Meet, the three aircraft were transferred to the newly activated 355th TFW at George.

36th TFW

The two "German" wings were notified by 17AF on June 29 that they would participate. With this late decision, they were already significantly behind with their preparations. With regard to the 36th TFW, its Deputy Commander of Operations (DCO), Col Carroll Stanton, then made hasty plans to select the best pilot to represent his Wing. Three pilots each from the 22nd, 23rd, and 53rd TFS, and two pilots from the Wing's Tactical Evaluation Division, were selected to deploy to Wheelus AB, Libya, for a competitive elimination. During the first two weeks of July, the 11 pilots flew an equal number of sorties, competing in, for example, "nuclear" deliveries, strafing, and dart air-to-air shooting. Eighteen sorties were flown each day. After the team had returned to Bitburg, the Wing commander, Col Delashaw, selected Capts John Ruffo (22nd TFS) and Phillip Bradley (53rd) to represent the 36th TFW as primary and alternate pilot, respectively. Capt Rod Giffin (22nd TFS) was appointed as the operations and maintenance officer. In addition, maintenance and support personnel were selected. On August 1, Ruffo and Bradley returned to Wheelus to practice for the Meet. In nine flying days,

37 sorties were flown with two specific F-105Ds. For instance, aircraft 05385 flew an average of 2.4 sorties per day on August 6–10.

It was initially intended that the team would fly their aircraft to Nellis. However, before they could do so, the F-105Ds had to go through Phase I of Look-Alike at Bitburg. When this was delayed, it was decided to pick up three new aircraft. The team flew to the US in a C-130. The Bitburg pilots arrived at Nellis on August 27 with three new Block 20RE F-105Ds. According to the 22nd TFS history, "For two weeks the team worked day and night trying to make the aircraft acceptable. They had to be bore-sighted, Doppler problems had to be solved, missing parts of the toss bomb computer were to be inserted, and broken pylons and wing wiring had to be redone." Also, "The pre-meet practice went very well, and when the competition started, all systems in the primary and backup aircraft were 'Go.'"

Ruffo flew all sorties without an abort and had the distinction of having the best simulated nuclear and best conventional sortie of any participant. However, his overall points total was low because of navigation and intelligence problems. For instance, his APN-131 Doppler did not work on any mission, and on one mission the wrong target coordinates had been given. After the competition, the F-105Ds were ferried to Bitburg.

49th TFW

The 49th TFW was also at Wheelus to select its primary and alternate pilot, but did so differently. Capt Mike Muskat said:

By the end of June, each of the 7th, 8th, and 9th TFS nominated one pilot based on the highest bombing and gunnery scores achieved by their members. I was on temporary duty (TDY) at Nellis

Aircraft of TAC's only F-104C wing, George's 479th TFW, were also present at WT 62. The primary Starfighter pilot, Capt Charles Tofferi, became the competition's Top Gun, collecting 19,018 out of a possible 24,000 points. (Lockheed)

at that time. When I returned to Spangdahlem, Col Dawson, the Wing's DCO told me to replace the nominee of the 9th TFS. I guess the fact that I was a graduate of the F-100 Fighter Weapons School had something to do with this. Later in July, the three of us and a maintenance team flew to Wheelus to compete for the top spot. The result was that I became the primary and Capt Lawrence Brehm (8th TFS) the alternate pilot. Additional training was also conducted at Wheelus. Altogether, much time, energy, and resources were expended.

The team, with Col John Groom as project officer, also flew across the Atlantic in a C-130 Hercules. According to Capt Muskat, "Like Bitburg, we could not take our best and carefully prepared F-105Ds, as they had not yet gone through the modification line. Also, TAC threatened to ground them after arrival in the US, as their F-105Ds were grounded. This meant we had to pick up three Thunderchiefs that had not been 'peaked up'." The three aircraft were flown to Spang after the competition.

Practice

On September 10, the pilots received a detailed briefing on the rules. The next three days were used to permit each competitor of the ten F-100D (five TAC, three USAFE, and two PACAF wings), one F-104C (TAC), and three F-105D wings to fly pre-meet familiarization and practice sorties. All sorties were confined to areas that precluded inadvertent compromise of the Meet's targets. The maintenance competition was held on September 14. September 15–22 was reserved for the actual Meet, with the first five days as flying days and, when necessary, the 20th and 21st for make-up sorties or sorties to be re-flown.

The 12 "general" events to be flown included four nuclear-bomb delivery sorties, one GAM-83 (with an inert warhead), one air-to-air gunnery sortie against a dart tow target, and two strafe sorties. An interesting note is that the Bitburg pilots had no previous GAM-83 practice in the F-105D. Martin Marietta, the missile's manufacturer, made the Martin trophy available. Capt R E Bishop of the 405th FW (Clark AB, Philippines), flying an F-100D, had a 100 percent score. All F-105D sorties were flown by the primary pilots. Flight line support to maintain the primary and spare F-105D included one maintenance officer, two crew chiefs, one assistant crew chief, three weapons specialists, and one officer or airman as desired.

Top Gun

The Meet's "Top Gun" was Capt Charles Tofferi of the 479th TFW (George), flying an F-104C Starfighter. Of the possible 24,000 points, he achieved 19,018. He was awarded the Gen Jesse H. Auton Trophy. Of the F-105 pilots, Capt Muskat won 6th place with 15,534 points, Capt Ruffo came 11th with 12,273, and Capt Gardecki was 13th with 10,125 points.

The conclusion came on September 22 with a tactical air power demonstration at Indian Springs that was attended by 10,000 people. F-105Ds were refueled by KC-135A tankers and were involved, for instance, in pathfinder bombing, simulated nuclear weapon attacks and air-to-ground rocketry. Unfortunately, the Meet was marred on September 18 by the loss of F-100D 53720 and its pilot after he misjudged the dive angle during a rocket-firing pass. It was the first loss since the USAF Fighter Weapons Meet started in 1949.

Due to the worsening situation in SEA, no USAF worldwide tactical gunnery and bombing competitions were conducted until early September 1981 when Nellis hosted Gunsmoke 81. No F-105s of the two units that were still flying the aircraft participated in any Gunsmoke events.

Chapter 6
Various Units in Pictures

Before a new aircraft joins the active forces, it has to be tested. This also applies to modifications for new equipment and weaponry. Sometimes, the modification is so extensive that the aircraft "deserves a promotion," for instance, in the case of the F-105F Wild Weasel, which was re-designated F-105G.

Prior to June 1958, testing of aircraft, subsystems and munitions was conducted in Phases. There were seven for the F-105, and Phase I (air worthiness and equipment functioning) and Phase III (design refinement) were conducted by RAC. For this purpose, aircraft were bailed from the USAF. Bailed aircraft were aircraft assigned to approved USAF contractors for the performance or support of research, development, or test programs for the USAF. The other five, including, for instance, Phase VII (operational suitability) were conducted by the USAF with (maintenance) assistance by RAC. Bases involved included Edwards (Air Force Flight Test Center, AFFTC), Eglin (Air Proving Ground Center, APGC) and Wright-Patterson (WADC), those organizations all being assigned to ARDC. In June 1958, a new concept of testing was introduced to obtain a more coordinated effort and user participation. Testing went from the Phase-concept at various ARDC Centers to three Categories (Cat) with just one Center to handle the complete project. Cat III, for instance, involved the OT&E (Operational Test and Evaluation) of the system and was a joint ARDC/user test, under the responsibility of the using command, which also prepared and coordinated the test plan, with contractor technical support as required.

Republic had facilities at both Edwards and Eglin. For instance, on August 1, 1969, then called Fairchild Hiller, Republic Aircraft Division (FH-RAD; Fairchild Hiller bought Republic in 1965) was working at Eglin on four different development programs on a two-shift basis, employing some 44 personnel, plus those temporary engineer-type personnel from Farmingdale. For this purpose, FH-RAD bailed two F-105D and two F-105F aircraft from the USAF. A fifth bailed aircraft, an F-105F, arrived on August 19. Such a program was Project Directive 4700Y80, Cat I developmental testing of the QRC-380, which included the final Class V modification to be issued to FH-RAD prior to termination of its operations at Eglin. The QRC-380 was a Westinghouse Electric Company electronic counter-measures system. For this purpose, two F-105Fs were bailed, 24422 and 24434. The project was accomplished in the July 1969–January 1970 period.

APGC, which was re-designated on August 1, 1968, as Armament Development and Test Center (ADTC), at Eglin was involved extensively in testing the systems and weaponry of the B, D, F and G models of the F-105, starting with the F-105B in 1957. The war in Southeast Asia and the problems with the F-105 increased the number of projects considerably. For instance, on June 30, 1966, APGC had 13 F-105s assigned, 1/F-105B, 10/JF-105D and 2/JF-105F for testing and test support. Test programs included F-105D contract Class V modifications tests, analysis of the mini-gun in the F-105 (and F-4), and F-105/QRC-160 ECM pod evaluation. On January 1, 1972, ADTC still had five F-105s in its inventory. However, the last one left Eglin on June 30.

Above: Project Fast Wind was USAF's effort at Edwards AFB to set a new world speed record for a 100-km closed circuit without payload. The aircraft involved was the F-105B, of which the 334th TFS provided two, 75812 (backup) and 75823 (primary). A world record (1,163.35mph), was set on December 11, 1959, by BG Joe Moore, commander of the 4th TFW. In the photo, BG Moore is in "823" before take-off on December 11. (via Joe Moore)

Right: The APGC at Eglin AFB had several (J)F-105D/Fs assigned for test work. Some of them were also temporarily bailed to Republic for their test work. The 1964 photo shows six (J)F-105Ds and one JF-105F. (USAF)

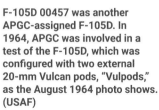

F-105D 00457 was another APGC-assigned F-105D. In 1964, APGC was involved in a test of the F-105D, which was configured with two external 20-mm Vulcan pods, "Vulpods," as the August 1964 photo shows. (USAF)

For the Look-Alike modifications, USAFE F-105Ds were returned to MOAMA at Brookley AFB and then flown back to Germany. With regard to the second major F-105 modification program, Safety Pack I and II, it was decided for several reasons not to return the aircraft to CONUS but to contract Construcciones Aeronáuticas, S.A. (CASA) at Getafe, Spain. CASA was already engaged in work of a parallel nature on other USAFE aircraft (F-100, F-102), and was considered competent and reliable. The first aircraft to go through Safety Pack Phase I was F-105F 38299 of the 49th TFW, which arrived on January 18, 1965. It was used as a prototype. All aircraft were to return to CASA for Phase II. This Phase was completed on July 29, 1966, when USAFE's 150th and last F-105D/F departed for its home base. The photo shows a CASA Getafe hangar with USAFE F-105D/Fs undergoing Safety Pack modifications. (Coll/TvG)

SMAMA at McClellan AFB was one of three Safety Pack modification lines in CONUS. The mid-April 1965 photo shows three F-105Ds and one F-105F undergoing Safety Pack I modification. (USAF)

Above: F-105D 10167 was assigned to APGC on August 22, 1962, when it was delivered to the USAF. It remained at Eglin until assignment to the 149th TFS at Byrd Field on February 12, 1973. The photo shows the aircraft at a cold Hill AFB, being prepared for an armament test mission at what is now known as the Utah Test and Training Range (UTTR). (Coll/TvG)

Right: 38362 was a straight F-105F of the 561st TFS and was at McClellan in May 1969 for IRAN (inspect and repair as necessary). Note the extended bomb bay tank. (TvG)

In the August 31, 1965–July 21, 1971, period, F-105D 24291 was used by SMAMA as a test-bed. Its first job was participation (October 25–December 23, 1965) in TAC Test 65-85A "Wild Weasel IA." For this purpose, "291" was configured with Applied Technology Inc. APR-25V RHAW equipment. A second system, the Bendix Pacific AN/DPN-61/Maxson, was tested on F-105D 10138. ATI's APR-25V was selected. The photo shows the aircraft at McClellan in May 1969. Note the open bomb bay. (TvG)

In general, F-105s that were used at Eglin as test-beds would be used as such for many years because of their specific modifications. For instance, F-105D 81173 arrived at Eglin on July 21, 1960, and until its assignment to the 121st TFS at Andrews on February 16, 1973, it was used by the APGC/ADTC (APGC was re-designated on August 1, 1968, as the Armament Development and Test Center (ADTC)) and as bailment to Republic. The June 12, 1971, photo shows "173" at Eglin in ADTC markings. (Remington)

When the F-105 was phased out, the majority of aircraft were flown to Davis-Monthan for storage at MASDC, which was re-designated in October 1985 as the Aerospace Maintenance and Regeneration Center. The first F-105 to arrive at MASDC was F-105D 10183 on July 6, 1973, from Tinker. A total of 95 F-105B/D/F/Gs would make their final trip to Davis-Monthan. The only F-105 left is G/38285, which is one of the aircraft on "Celebrity Row." (TvG)

With the retirement of the F-105 Thunderchief, many examples began a new life in the ABDR training program under deployment conditions. This photo shows five of those aircraft, four Bs and one Thunderstick II D. They were all assigned to the 2954th CLSS at Kelly AFB but "stationed" at the Army's Camp Bullis. (John Kerr)

Chapter 7
Operational Readiness Inspection

The first indication that PACAF was to receive F-105s came in July 1958 when 5AF informed 313AD that its subordinate 18th TFW at Kadena, on Okinawa, would be re-equipped with three F-105 squadrons, beginning in the October–December 1961 period. The 5AF information was based on a program document received from USAF, which reflected revised F-105 production rates detained from Republic. An initial F-105 Weapon Systems Phasing meeting was held on February 9–10, 1959, by the Air Materiel Force Pacific at Headquarters PACAF in Hawaii. Several meetings followed in which a PACAF operations concept and requirements for the F-105 were established. On February 25, the 5AF Weapons System Phasing Committee held its first meeting, which included a briefing on the characteristics of the F-105 and its planned deployment in the PACAF theater. On March 7, 1960, PACAF issued its Programmed Action Directive (PAD) 60-2, "F-105D Conversion 18th TFW" with the objective of a timely and coordinated scheduling of actions required to convert the Wing from F-100D/F to F-105D aircraft. It showed, for instance, that the 12th TFS would be the first unit to convert, in the April–June 1962 period. Several revisions of PAD 60-2 followed.

PACAF's first four F-105Ds on the flight line at Hickam after arriving from Nellis on October 23. Only three arrived at Kadena one week later with 10169 staying behind at Hickam with maintenance problems. (USAF)

When the three Thunderchiefs approached Okinawa they were picked up by four F-100s, RF-101s, and F-102s, which escorted the F-105s to their new home. (USAF)

The conversion to the F-105 became more serious on April 10, 1961, when the 18th TFW established an F-105 project office that would be responsible for all planning and coordination to assure as smooth a transition as possible during the conversion. The project officer was to function as a special assistant to the Wing commander.

F-105 training at Kadena was initiated in February 1962 by Field Training Detachment (FTD) 911A. By 30 June, all personnel intended for duty with the new aircraft had received training. The first 11 pilots, all from the 67th TFS, the first unit to convert, departed on April 10 for Nellis for F-105D upgrade training. They returned on June 10, however, without the "promised" aircraft due to a strike at RAC in Farmingdale and groundings.

Augmentation

As a total of 15 SIOP targets would be left uncovered during the conversion period (in addition to the 18th, the 8th TFW at Itazuke, in Japan, would also convert to F-105Ds from F-100D/Fs), PACAF, through CINCPAC (Commander-in-Chief, Pacific) requested that the Joint Chiefs of Staff (JCS) on January 27, 1962, approve the rotation of a TAC tactical fighter squadron to PACAF in the May 1, 1962–June 30, 1963, period. TAC was amenable to the proposal and told PACAF, assuming the request would be approved, that one F-105B squadron, complete with flyaway kit, would deploy to Kadena May 1962–January 1963 as augmentation to maintain the SIOP posture. This squadron would then be replaced by an F-105D squadron until June 1963 for the conversion at Itazuke. On March 16, the JCS directed the Commander-in-Chief, US Strike Forces (CINCSTRIKE) to release a TFS to USAF for further assignment to PACAF. Simultaneously, USAF was instructed to take immediate action required to augment the Pacific forces by one rotational TFS to support PACAF's conversion to the F-105D, during May 1, 1962–June 30, 1963. The next turn in the process was TAC's, which tasked the 31st TFW at George to deploy its F-100D/F Super Sabre-equipped 306th TFS for the commitment, rather than a Seymour Johnson-based F-105B squadron as had first been planned. Upon deployment of the first squadron, TAC would plan to conduct personnel-type rotations throughout the 14 months; the aircraft would remain, with personnel rotating every three months. TAC's plan was approved by USAF. In the meantime, the 18th TFW had initiated the redeployment of its first Super Sabres to CONUS.

On April 4, 1962, Col Frank Collins, the 31st TFW commander, visited Kadena to arrange for the TDY, and a tentative support agreement, drawn up at Headquarters PACAF on April 5–6, was subsequently reviewed at TAC and 12AF. The agreement included that: (1) PACAF would assume operational control and logistic responsibility at 140°W longitude; (2) the deployment would include 192 personnel, including 24 aircrews; (3) the 18 F-100D/Fs would deploy with 450-gallon fuel tanks installed; and (4) equipment would include seven spare engines.

Retraining

After notification of the deployment, the 306th TFS immediately began an intensive in-flight refueling training program with TAC KB-50J Superfortress aircraft. However, on April 13, USAF directed SAC to utilize its KC-135A Stratotankers to refuel the Super Sabres en route George–Hickam AFB, Hawaii. From there, PACAF would assume responsibility with its KB-50Js. TAC could not support the deployment with its own KB-50Js due to the extremely heavy maintenance requirement, imposed after the loss of a KB-50J tanker over the Atlantic earlier in the year. For the 306th, the switch to KC-135As resulted in retraining.

Aborted

The deployment was initiated on April 18–22, when C-118s and C-124s of the Military Air Transport Service, carrying equipment and tactical support elements, departed George for Kadena. At the same time, the 18th TFW sent movement control teams to Wake Island and Andersen AFB, Guam, to assist the 306th TFS on its deployment. The 306th TFS, as *Lima Mike 1*, began its deployment on April 24, when 18 primary and four spare F-100D/Fs left George for the first leg to Hickam, supported by SAC KC-135As. Four days later, 14 of the aircraft arrived at Kadena, while two had aborted at Midway and

F-105D 10165 "Jake's Jewel" touching down on October 30 on Kadena's runway. (Frank Street)

The arrival ceremony for the first three F-105Ds. On the "carpet" MG Robert Stillman (313AD commander) is giving his welcoming speech with the pilots and their wives as a serious audience. (USAF)

two at Wake where their maintenance problems were fixed by ESTs (en-route support teams). On May 5, the 15 Ds and three Fs had arrived at Kadena. After target study was completed, six pilots and aircraft were committed to the alert force. Of note is the fact that while on rotation to Kadena, TAC Movement Order 4, published on March 29, 1962, changed the home station of the 31st TFW with its subordinate units, including the 306th, from George to Homestead AFB, Florida, on July 1, 1962. The 306th cross-switched with the 309th TFS on July 17 (*Lima Mike 2*) and returned to their new home station.

October

Although PACAF announced in August 1962 that the 18th TFW would receive its first four F-105Ds in September, the next 12 in October, 14 in November, and an additional 17 in December, this proved to be too optimistic. When September rolled around, the information vouchsafed by the Command was that the first aircraft would not be received until October. This proved to be correct, although Kadena had to wait until the next to last day of that month to welcome the first three aircraft. The planning had been for the arrival of four aircraft, but one remained at Hickam due to maintenance problems. The aircraft had been flown from the RAC facility to MOAMA at Brookley AFB, where they were prepared for the flight to Kadena through aircraft assignment directives (AADs) 2-2646 and -2653 of October 3 and 4, respectively. The 4440th ADG was responsible for the ferry, for which the Pacific *Flying Fish* route was used. After a stop at Nellis and George, the aircraft arrived at Hickam on October 23 and adorned with nicknames: 10163, "Tommy's Hawk"; 10165, "Jake's Jewel"; 10169, "The Moose Mobile"; and 10171, "The Irish Rose." Via Andersen, 10163, 10165, and 10171 arrived at Kadena on October 30 with Col George Simler, the Wing commander, in "171," touching down first. The other two pilots were Capts Marty Mahrt and Lloyd Anders, both of the 67th TFS. A Wing F-100D escorted the three F-105s from Andersen to Kadena. Near the base, they were met and escorted by four-ship flights of F-100s, RF-101 Voodoos, and F-102 Delta Daggers, the latter from Naha AB, Okinawa. The gala welcome included a band, an honor guard, and welcoming speeches by MG Robert Stillman (313AD commander) and Col Simler, after which the spectators were allowed to inspect the long-awaited Thunderchiefs. The acceptance inspections of the three F-105Ds in the week after the arrival showed with regard to Col Simler's F-105D that a wheel had been installed incorrectly.

In the meantime, due to the Cuban Missile Crisis, DEFCON 3 for US forces was implemented worldwide on October 23. At Kadena, flyable alert F-100Ds were uploaded and placed on ground alert status, bringing the total number of static alert aircraft to 24. On November 16, the Wing returned to normal alert status.

Schedule of target assumption

Targets	F-105D	F-100D	TAC F-100D
Nov 1962	0/0/0*	12/6/5*	6/0/6*
Jan 1963	2/2/0	10/4/5	6/0/6
Apr 1963	12/6/5	0/0/0	6/0/6
Jul 1963	18/6/31	0/0/0	0/0/0

* respectively, QS= Quick Strike/FA=Flyable Alert/NA=Non-Alert

Non-stop

On the first day of 1963, the 18th TFW had 43 F-105Ds assigned, plus 36 F-100Ds, six F-100Fs, 18 RF-101Cs, 14 T-33As, five C-47s, and two C-54s. A tentative date to assume the first F-105D targets was met; on January 7, 1963, the first SIOP targets were assumed by Quick Strike F-105Ds. The pickup of the target commitment was also met as scheduled, with F-105Ds covering 45 assigned targets on June 15. This meant that the support of the TDY 308th TFS was no longer necessary with the resulting move to Itazuke to support the conversion of the 8th TFW.

On February 10, Col Jones Bolt, the Wing's vice commander, and Capt James Malone of the 67th TFS landed their Thunderchiefs at Kadena after making the first non-stop flight from Hickam to Okinawa in a single-engine aircraft. It took them some 5,300 miles and 9hrs 52mins. The course took them from Hickam to Wake Island and Guam. The first aerial refueling was 635 miles east of Honolulu, the second over Wake Island, and the third and last one, 43 miles east of Guam. In-flight lunch had been prepared at Hickam with the food particles compressed into cube size.

Parade

The 83rd and final F-105D for the wing, 24269, arrived on March 24 as part of a three-ship. This did not mean all Super Sabres had left. Three F-100Ds, assigned to Base Flight, were retained to fly tow missions with the dart target until an approved F-105 tow rig was available. On April 6, the 18th TFW conducted a formal parade in honor of eight wing members who were awarded the Air Force Commendation Medal. About 1,500 officers and airmen passed in review with LG Paul Caraway, High Commissioner US Civil Administration of the Ryukyu Islands, as the reviewing officer. Sixteen F-105Ds conducted a flyover to signal the start of the parade. The Thunderchiefs flew by in the form of an "18," while five Voodoos underlined the numbered formation to their rear. In addition, Mrs George Simler champagne-christened F-105D 24269 *Freedom Warrior*.

C-1 Status

It had been anticipated during the October 18–19, 1962, Conversion Conference that the Wing would attain its C-1 OR date on May 20, 1963, 90 days after receipt of 70 percent of the authorized number of aircraft. Minimum C-1 standards were 86 aircrews formed with 81 being Combat Ready (CR).

The arrival of the first F-105Ds meant that maintenance personnel could finally work on a real aircraft. The instrument on the ground is an F-105 armament test set. (USAF)

Sixty-four aircraft were to be possessed with 53 being OR. An operational readiness inspection (ORI) would take place within 90 days after the 18th TFW had attained at least a C-2 status (60 aircrews formed with 55 CR and 46 aircraft to be possessed with 38 being OR). PACAF PAD 60-2C (Revised) of December 6, 1962, changed the date to June 30, 1963. However, as the Wing had failed to qualify sufficient aircrews, the new C-1 date was not met. The primary reason was the training time lost as a result of two typhoon evacuations conducted during June, the first on June 10 for Typhoon Rose and the second on June 16 for Typhoon Shirley. To expedite aircrew qualifications, the 18th borrowed an additional F-100 for dart tow purposes, and Saturday and holiday flying was initiated. It was expected that typhoons and/ or other extended adverse weather would stay away from Okinawa in July, and the C-1 status would be reached by July 31. On July 13, Typhoon Wendy resulted in "condition III" being declared. When this was upgraded the next day to "condition II," 66 F-105Ds were evacuated. "All clear" was proclaimed on July 15 and all aircraft returned to Kadena. On that same date, the Wing had enough qualified aircrews to attain a C-1 status. Fifth Air Force then reported to PACAF that the 18th TFW was C-1 as of 24:00, July 31. In August, the three remaining F-100Ds (53562, -564, and -580) left for Clovis AFB, New Mexico, after towing had been assumed by F-105Ds, while the final F-100, F-100F 81209, departed on September 18.

"Big" Day

An ORI evaluates the degree of readiness of a combat unit, for instance a TFW. It is always an exciting event, especially after a conversion. The 18th TFW was the fifth operational wing to convert to the

F-105 Thunderchief. The first one was the 4th TFW at Seymour Johnson. The second and third wings were the 36th and 49th at Bitburg and Spangdahlem AB, respectively. The 355th TFW at George was a newly activated wing, which received its first three F-105Ds on September 28, 1962.

August 8 proved to be the "big" day when 25 members of the PACAF "Bearcat" ORI Team, led by Col James Wilson, arrived at Kadena, augmented by Standardization and Evaluation, and flying safety officers of other PACAF units. Although the 15th Tactical Reconnaissance Squadron, Photo-Jet, at Kadena was attached to the 18th TFW and assigned to the 313AD, it was included in the ORI. The inspection consisted of four phases: (1) the wing's capability to react to recall personnel and to generate aircraft in accordance with the General War Plans (GWP). This opening phase was directed by practice emergency action messages; (2) to test its ability to simulate a GWP profile and bombing mission; (3) to test its ability to load and deliver conventional weapons in a contingency role; and (4) supervisory and managerial inspections. At 10:15, the Wing Command Center received a situation message, which was intended to simulate the "strategic warning." At 18:00, MG Albert Clark, 313AD commander, declared defense condition "Round House." Immediately, all F-105Ds were placed in a position and configured to accept a war reserve weapon, ie, two 450-gallon fuel tanks installed on the inboard pylons with the bomb bay being prepared to load the weapon.

A-hour, the alert hour, was announced the next day at 05:00. The F-105s were quickly loaded for bear and the ORI Team chief directed a simulated alert of the high-alert gear force, which was executed within the prescribed time. The quick-strike alert pilots assumed a cockpit alert status, which lasted two hours, after which they returned to their normal operations. The non-alert aircraft were generated on the main parking ramp but were not moved to a runway alert position. These aircraft were configured with (empty) 650-gallon fuselage tanks. At 09:00, the 18 quick-strike pilots returned to their cockpits. Thirty-nine minutes later, a PACAF message was received, establishing "E" hour as 10:00. Six minutes later, the J-75 engines of the 18 aircraft were started after receiving a red flare signal from the Emergency Operations Element at the runway control position. The generated non-alert aircraft simulated "start engines" as required by the inspectors. At A+4:33, 55 aircraft were required and, based on pilot acceptance, 55 were available.

The launch of 55 aircraft was involved in Phase II. It included a simulated GWP profile (high/low) mission and the dropping of a BDU-8 practice bomb on the Ie Shima bombing range. The BDU-8 was carried in

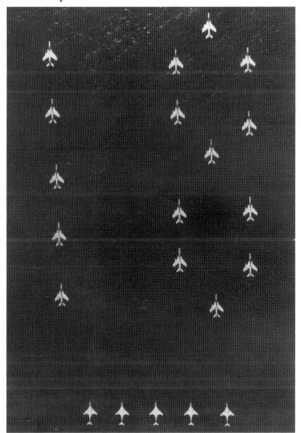

On April 6, the 18th TFW conducted a formal parade. Sixteen F-105Ds conducted a flyover to signal the start of the parade. The Thunderchiefs flew by in the form of an "18," while five Voodoos underlined the numbered formation to its rear. (USAF)

Also on April 6, Mrs George Simler champagne-christened F-105D 24269 *Freedom Warrior*, the final F-105D for the Wing, which had arrived on March 24. (USAF)

the bomb bay. The route distance was 493 nautical miles, the last 200 of which had to be flown low level. Five of the pilots were required to use the thermal shield as a hood, to fly the last 100 nautical miles at 2,000 feet, and deliver the weapon while under the hood. These five sorties were chased by ORI Team pilots. The result: 55 sorties required, 55 flown with 52 being successful; 55 radar deliveries required and 48 flown.

Phase III, flown on August 14–18, consisted of a number of different missions, including: (1) 36 air-to-ground sorties were required and flown. The configuration was two 450-gallon fuel tanks on the inboards, two LAU-3 rocket pods with nine rockets each on the outboards, an MN-1A bomb dispenser on the centerline station, an MD-6 center section in the bomb bay for ballast, and 300 rounds of 20-mm ammunition. Each sortie consisted of two skip-bomb, one rocket, two dive-bomb, and two strafing passes; (2) 36 dart sorties scheduled and flown. The configuration was two 450-gallon tanks on the inboards, the MD-6 in the bomb bay and 300 rounds of 20-mm ammunition. Each pilot was allowed two passes at the dart; (3) 12 GAR-8 Sidewinder sorties scheduled and flown. A configuration of two 450-gallon tanks on the inboards, GAR-8 pylons on the outboards with the Sidewinder on the right outboard, and the target rocket on the left outboard, plus the MD-6. Nine missiles successfully hit their targets; and (4) four F-105Ds were configured to fly a conventional strike mission with live ordnance. Configuration was as follows: two aircraft with six M-117 750-pound bombs on the centerline MER, two 450-gallon tanks on the inboards, and two LAU-3A rocket pods with 19 rockets each; one F-105D with six LAU-3A pods with 114 rockets; and one aircraft with four M-116 fire bombs, and two LAU-3A pods with 19 rockets each. After take-off, the ordnance was delivered on Range 176. Scoring was accomplished by an airborne ORI Team member. Running concurrently with the flying evaluation was Phase IV, evaluation of all areas of the Wing's operations, maintenance, supporting functions, and administration.

The average aircraft in-commission rate was 85.7 percent with 80 percent required. Although there were no maintenance-charged aborts on mission aircraft, maintenance was charged with four aborts involving chase aircraft. A total of 213 sorties were flown, including four functional check flights (FCFs), for 285 flying hours. There were 11 ground and five air aborts. The 12th TFS was "high" overall and had a "high" pilot in both "nuclear" and conventional deliveries. When the ORI Team left Kadena on August 17, the 18th TFW had become the very first F-105 wing to pass an ORI with a C-1 rating: fully operationally ready. The overall rating was "satisfactory." The few minor discrepancies that had been found were quickly corrected. On August 29, the Air Force Chief of Staff (CSAF), Gen Curtis LeMay, sent the 18th TFW a letter of congratulations for its record conversion to the F-105 and passing the subsequent ORI.

Epilogue

After the 355th TFW at Takhli RTAB had transferred its F-105D/Fs to McConnell AFB, Kansas, in October 1970, for flyable storage and to the 18th TFW, the 12th TFS became the sole squadron in PACAF that was equipped with the D/F version of the F-105. However, two months later, the Squadron had lost many of its combat-ready aircrews in an action to reduce it in total size. The number of F-105s had dropped from a high of 39 to 21. In June 1971, the 12th had 14 line pilots and 16 aircraft (14 Ds and two Fs). On July 1, F-4Cs took over the ground alert at Kadena from the F-105Ds.

In January 1972, the 12th still had 13 F-105s, all Ds. The Squadron was relieved of all alert commitments. On March 8, F-105D 24399 was lost while on an air-to-ground gunnery mission on the Ie Shima range. Pilot and aircraft were not recovered. Although a plan had been implemented on November 11, 1971, to convert the 12th TFS to A-7D Corsair IIs, the conversion was cancelled on March 11, 1972. Most of the squadron pilots already had class dates to attend A-7 upgrading. Instead, on March 22, the 18th TFW was directed to transfer the F-105s to CONUS, which would result in the inactivation of the Squadron. One week later, all flight training requirements were dropped and only FCFs, acceptance flights, and necessary instrument checks could be accomplished. On April 12, all local flying was terminated and the first flight of four F-105Ds (91729, 24259, 24284, and 24346) departed Kadena, followed five days later by the second flight of four Ds (24279, 24301, 24328, and 24348). Although the third flight was also supposed to have four F-105Ds, it had only three when the return to the US was initiated on April 27. Six days earlier, Capt Bill Thomas was lost south of Ie Shima while on a sortie in F-105D 24244 to check the aircraft prior to its overwater flight to the US on April 24. Significant parts of "244" were recovered but the pilot was not. Two days later, a memorial service was held at Kadena with the three remaining F-105Ds (24248, 24360, and 24372) flying a missing man formation. The departure of the final three Ds marked the end of an era in Pacific operations. Seven of the aircraft were flown to Sacramento Air Materiel Area (SMAMA) at McClellan, California, for major overhaul, and four were flown to their new home, the 465th TFS at Tinker AFB, Oklahoma.

Under Project PAF 4F-128, F-105Fs were ferried to the 8th at Itazuke and 18th TFW at Kadena. On May 4, 1964, the first four two-seaters arrived at Kadena under AAD 4-957. (USAF)

After the 18th TFW had been directed on March 22, 1972, to transfer its F-105Ds to the US, eight departed Kadena in the April 12–17 period. This left the Wing's 12th TFS with the final four Ds and an April 24 departure date. However, on April 21, Capt Thomas and his F-105D 24244 were lost on a sortie south of Ie Shima while checking the aircraft prior to its overwater flight. The photo shows "244" at Yokota in March 1971. (H. Nagakubo)

After the loss of Capt Thomas, the departure of the last three aircraft was delayed until April 27. Their departure, including 24372, marked the end of an era in Pacific operations. (Coll/TvG)

Chapter 8

Pacific Air Forces in Pictures

The 8th TFW at Itazuke AB was the second PACAF wing to convert to the F-105D. It was initiated on January 2, 1963. As a result of Project Clearwater, the realignment of forces in the Pacific area, its three tactical fighter squadrons (35th, 36th, and 80th) moved to Yokota AB and were reassigned to the 41AD, while the 8th TFW designator was moved to George AFB. When the 6441st TFW was designated and organized at Yokota on April 1, 1965, the three squadrons were reassigned to the new wing. On November 15, 1966, the wing was discontinued and inactivated, with the squadrons re-joining the 41AD. This was changed once more when they were reassigned to the 347th TFW when this Wing was organized at Yokota on January 15, 1968. At that moment, the 80th TFS was the only unit still flying the F-105. The 4440th ADG was also responsible for *Flying Fish*, the ferry of aircraft across the Pacific, and "hired" pilots to fly them. The photo shows four of those pilots, three of the 44th and one of the 35th TFS. F-105D 24303 was delivered in April 1963 to the 8th TFW at Itazuke. (Ed Skowron)

F-105D 24373 was delivered to Itazuke in September 1963. (Gene Van Houten)

Above: F-105Ds 24377 and 24380 are being refueled by TAC KB-50J 0-90352 of the 431st Air Refueling Squadron while on an October 1963 *Flying Fish* ferry from George to Hickam. The ultimate destination was Itazuke. (USAF)

Left: The Japanese-based F-105Ds pulled SIOP alert at Osan AB. The photo shows F-105D 24387 of the 8th TFW taking off from Osan. (Larry Van Pelt)

Below: F-105D 24346 of the 80th TFS was one of the final batch of F-105s that departed Itazuke for Yokota in May 1964. The text, which includes "Yokota or Bust" tells it all. (Marty Case)

F-105D 24360 of the 80th TFS (yellow intake) on a ferry flight in the company of KC-135A 23558. (Coll/TvG)

After it had been decided to centralize maintenance, the F-105D/Fs lost their individual squadron markings, and their tails were adorned with wing colors. On this photo, made during *Pacific Concord I*, F-105F 38294 has the 6441st TFW colors on the tail: blue/yellow/red for the 35th, 80th, and 36th, respectively. (Jim Brown)

Weapon technicians are installing a CBU-2A/A dispenser on F-105D 24375 of the 6441st TFW at RAAF Williamtown during Exercise *Pacific Concord I*, October 4–17, 1965. (USAF)

Of the three F-105Ds on this December 1966 photo, only 00522 still lacks the RHAW equipment. The snow-covered mountain in the background is Mount Fuji. (Les Sundt)

The 80th TFS was the last F-105 squadron stationed in Japan and the only one flying Thuds with the unit tail code "GR." When the *Pueblo* Crisis began, the unit deployed the F-105s to Osan where they were eventually absorbed by the 12th TFS. This January 29, 1968, photo shows F-105D 10175 on its ferry flight to Osan. (Dick Smith)

October 18–27, 1963, the 18th TFW sent ten F-105Ds to Kung Kuan AB, Republic of China, to participate in Exercise *Sky Soldier/Tien Bing IV*. The 67th TFS was the responsible unit. Its aircraft were utilized as aggressors, while PACAF F-100D/Fs and Chinese F-104 and F-86 aircraft acted as friendly forces. The photo shows three of the F-105s, including 24284 of Red Section (67th TFS). (Frank Street)

F-105D 24235 of Red Section returning to Kadena after flying a training sortie. (Frank Street)

Armament for the two PACAF F-105D wings also included the Martin Marietta GAM-83 Bullpup, which was re-designated AGM-12 in June 1963. In this stunning photo, the pilot of F-105F 38282 of Yellow Section (12th TFS) has just launched an AGM-12B and is using a control joystick to steer it to the target. (Dag Damewood)

F-105D 10204 and F-105F 38278 in the company of two RF-101C Voodoos and a KC-135A. Note that "278" is still without RHAW gear. (John Rehm)

At the time of the seizure by the North Koreans of the USS *Pueblo*, PACAF had five F-4Cs on SIOP alert at Osan and Kunsan. The seizure resulted in deployment on January 23 of 12 F-105Ds and on January 29 of another 12 F-105D/Fs of the 12th TFS from Kadena to Osan. After arrival, the aircraft were immediately uploaded with six M-117 bombs on the centerline MER (multiple ejection rack) and two AIM-9Bs on dual launchers on each outboard station. On the photo, a 12th TFS F-105D is configured with six M-117s and two AIM-9B Sidewinders. (USAF)

Chapter 9

The Thunderchief's Final Episode

After the 39th TFTS at George AFB had transferred its F-105F/G functions to the 562nd TFS on June 1, 1978, the latter became the sole operator within the 35th TFW and the active Air Force to operate the F-105 Thunderchief. This meant the Squadron would also train F-105G aircrews, including those for the 128th TFS of the Georgia ANG at Dobbins AFB, which would convert from F-100D/F Super Sabres to F-105F/Gs. Between September 13 and 20, 1978, the first four F-105Gs were transferred to Dobbins.

Thud Sawadee

On June 27, 1980, the last active-duty operational F-105 Thunderchief mission was flown. Its callsign was "Thud" with F/38343, Maj "Wild Bill" Kennedy/Capt George Armstrong as Thud 01; G/38285, Maj Ken Thaete/Capt Thomas Tedford as Thud 02; and G/24446, Maj Jimmy Boyd/Capt Larry Ware as Thud 03.

To commemorate the departure of the F-105 from the active USAF inventory July 11–13, 1980, Tactical Training, George published OPORD 04-80, "Thud Sawadee." Friendly forces included the 35th TFW, the four ANG F-105 units (121st, 128th, 141st, and 149th TFS) and the three Air Force Reserve (AFRes) squadrons (457th, 465th, and 466th TFS). Events included an open house, including, for example, a static display of all F-105 models configured with inert munitions; a flyby of all F-105 models, led by the 562nd TFS; and a party for maintenance personnel. In addition, F-105G 24416 was

To commemorate the departure of the F-105 from the active Air Force's inventory, Tactical Training, George organized the Thud Sawadee on July 11–13, 1980. One of the events was a flyby of all F-105 models, led by an F-105G of the 562nd TFS (38285). The other aircraft were an F-105B (75776, 141st TFS), F-105D (24372, 465th TFS), F-105D Thunderstick II (00490, 457th TFS), and F-105F (24413, 149th TFS). (USAF)

On October 8, TAC's last "Real Thunder" took place when the last two 35th TFW F-105Gs, 24446 and 38274, took off from George, heading for the 128th TFS. The photo shows "446" on an earlier training sortie. (TvG)

dedicated. The aircraft was involved in a class B mishap in September 1978 while employed at Karup AB, Denmark; it redeployed to George and had not flown since October 1978.

Throughout September 1980, another four F-105Gs were transferred to Dobbins, with the final two to follow. TAC's last "Real Thunder" took place on October 8, when the last two 35th TFW F-105s took off from George at 09:30L heading for the 128th TFS. The callsign was "Thud" with Maj Jimmy Boyd/ Lt Col Jim Padgett as 01 in G/24446 and Maj John Strawbridge/Capt Thomas Tedford as 02 in G/38274. Maj Jimmy Boyd was one of those "shit-hot" fighter pilots, who sometimes did not do things according to the book and got away with it. Jimmy said:

The acting Deputy Commander of Operations had permitted only to fly down the runway at 500 feet and 350 knots after we had taken off. However, we made a flyby over the ramp, low, and I mean low, at 600 knots, popping the burner and pulling up straight. The F-105 maintenance guys were all out on the ramp in front of our hangar and just loved it. They could feel the heat from the burner. The Supervisor of Flying in the tower said we were below the tower, 50 feet, when we flew by it.

According to Boyd, they were saved from court martial. Jim Padgett was the high-time F-105F/G EWO with 2,382 flying hours (the next EWO on the list had more than 400 fewer hours).

One day later, the Squadron was re-designated as a TFTS. The 562nd TFS delivered 11 F-105s to MASDC (Military Aircraft Storage and Disposition Center) at Davis-Monthan AFB for flyable storage, while 27 F-105F/Gs were transferred to the 128th TFS.

Seven

This left F-105s assigned to four ANG and three AFRes squadrons. One was to convert to Ling-Temco-Vought A-7D/K Corsair IIs, five to F-4D Phantoms, and one to F-16A/B Fighting Falcons. Kansas ANG's 127th TFTS had converted from F-105D/Fs to F-4Ds prior to the Thud Sawadee. The 128th TFS was the final ANG squadron to lose its Thunderchiefs on May 25, 1983, with the 466th TFS "Diamondback" remaining the last AFRes unit. Of interest is the fact that the 466th converted from the F-105B to the F-105D/F as late as October 1, 1980, receiving most of its Ds from the 465th TFS.

Long-term planning for the Squadron's conversion to the F-16A/B, a first for AFRes, had already been in progress since early 1982. It called for the transition to take place in early 1984 and for the retirement of the F-105 aircraft for storage at MASDC. The F-16 pre-SATAF (Site Activation Task

Force) planning conference took place at Hill on July 28–30, 1982. The conversion would result in an increase of 179 reserve military positions and $1.2m in military construction projects. Maintenance training was to begin in April 1983, primarily at Lowry AFB, Colorado, and formal aircrew training in July 1983 at Luke, Arizona. Two F-16s were scheduled to be available in October 1983 for hands-on maintenance training. Furthermore, the formal conversion date milestone was January 1, 1984, and 18 F-16A/Bs were to be received in 1984, with an additional six later.

Checkout

Condor Taco 83 at Kirtland AFB on January 8–22, 1983, was the last major F-105 deployment. It was the third consecutive time since January 1981 that the required annual active duty training took place at the New Mexican base. The deployment involved 12 F-105D/Fs, pilots and 350 reservists.

On March 14, Maj Glen Jepsen, the Wing safety officer, got the fright of his life. While flying at 500 feet on the UTTR, he experienced a severe bird strike. A rough-legged hawk broke through his canopy at the left windscreen, shattering the front screen and taking away Jepsen's forward view. He declared an emergency, returned to Hill and was able to land the aircraft safely.

March 15 saw the publication of TAC/AFRes PP 83-1, "419TFW (AFRes) F-16 Conversion." It programmed tasks, assigned responsibilities, and provided guidance for the preparation of detailed plans to accomplish, for example, equipping the 419th TFW/466th TFS with 18 Block 10 F-16A/B aircraft to be gained from the 56th and 388th TFW.

Capt Dave Perry became the very last pilot to be checked out in the F-105 on April 1, when he made his first solo landing. In late April, Air Training Command (ATC) sent a message to the 419th TFW, the parent unit of the 466th TFS, stating that USAF had established Project ATC 3F-073, assigning ten F-105Ds to the Air Force Military Training Center (AFMTC) at Lackland AFB, Texas, for use in the training program of security policemen in securing a flight line. A Wing technician was to deploy temporarily to Lackland to de-arm the aircraft.

In the May 16–20, 1983, period, the 419th TFW participated in Fighter Comp 83 at Gulfport ANG Training Site. Five hundred reservists represented 23 units in 17 states. Sixty tactical fighters participated, six each from ten 10AF units, flying F-105D, F-4D, and A-10A aircraft against targets at the Camp Shelby air-to-ground gunnery range. To practice for the competition, flying training during the April Unit Training Assembly (UTA) at Hill had consisted of six flights of four F-105Ds each, flying low-level timing and weapons delivery at Eagle Range. The results helped in determining the team members for Fighter Comp 83. Weather permitted the flying of three of the four planned competition missions. According to the Wing's history, "The 466th team placed second in their category,

Georgia's 128th TFS became the final ANG squadron to lose its Thunderchiefs on May 25, 1983, while converting to the F-4D. In the photo, the final ANG F-105, F/38299, is accompanied by F-4D 67662. Don Spering not only designed the special color scheme of "299," but also applied it to the F. (Don Spering/AIR)

Elephant walks have come into fashion among USAF units recently. However, the 466th TFS at Hill already did one on June 4, 1983, when maintenance was able to launch all 25 F-105s to execute a 24-aircraft flyby (21 Ds and three Fs) with a fourth F, 38365, being the photo ship. (via Kent Clark)

commendable considering the technological superiority of the A-10 and F-4." The wing's bomb loading crew had to load six Mk-82 500-pound bombs in less than 40 minutes and had the best individual load, turning in the fastest time and fewest errors. During the May 17–19 Safety Conference at Norton AFB, California, it was announced that the 466th was one of the three AFRes units to win a Flying Safety Award for 1982.

Reassignment

Retirement of the F-105 was initiated during the UTA of June 4–5. Four days earlier, Air Force Logistics Command (AFLC) had issued AAD 83-458, reassigning the first six of ten F-105Ds to the AFMTC at Lackland. Their "CC" combat mission code would be changed to the "TX" training mission code. AAD 83-723 of September 29 reassigned the other four aircraft, two on October 3 and two on October 12.

On June 4, maintenance was able to launch all 25 F-105s to execute a 24-aircraft flyby (21 Ds and three Fs) with a fourth F, 38365, being the photo ship. Retired Col Leo Thorsness flew in the back seat of F 38287. Col Thorsness, a Medal of Honor recipient and former prisoner of war in Hanoi, was credited with a MiG-17 kill on April 19, 1967, while flying Wild Weasel F-105F 38301. He stated, "It was marvelous to see all those Thuds out there. I thought we would sink the sky." The tribute was proposed on March 5 by Maj Terry Paasch, the Wing's Deputy Commander for Maintenance, and approved on March 22 by the Wing commander, Col Jonathan Gardner. Lt Col Bane Lyle, the Squadron commander, led the gaggle in F-105F 38309. Take-off was at close interval just after 10:00L, followed by a "diamonds-on-diamonds" flyover of Hill. Next was a mass strike training mission at Wildcat Tactical Gunnery Range. Nineteen aircraft then returned to Hill, while six Ds were refueled by Utah ANG KC-135Es on their way to Kelly AFB, Texas. After landing, the aircraft were towed to Lackland, which did not have an active runway.

In the period June 14–17, *Sea Saw 83* was conducted at Hill. It was a composite force training exercise, sponsored by the 388th TFW. The 466th was part of the Blue Strike Force, which also included F-111s, A-7s, and F-4s. Most of the Blue Force sorties were flown against Red Force runways, missile sites, anti-aircraft bunkers, and convoys, which were being protected by Marine Corps F/A-18s, and Air Force F-5s and F-15s. UH-1s retrieved Blue Force pilots placed out on the range to simulate combat rescue and recovery operations. The *Red Flag* exercise held at Nellis AFB July 16–29 witnessed the final participation of the F-105 Thunderchief. The 466th TFS flew 110 hours in 85 sorties. Eighteen F-105D/Fs remained on September 30. The number was 14 (10/D and 4/F) on December 31. On this date, no pilots were in F-105 upgrade training.

The October 1–2 UTA was the last during which F-105 aircraft were flown to Eagle Range as part of a squadron "Turkey Shoot." The top pilot was Maj Carl Womack. On October 12, Maj Jim Caldwell flew an F-105 to McClellan AFB, California, on a humanitarian sortie. Support was requested by the Red Cross of Salt Lake City, Utah, to help move a rare blood type to a critically ill patient in Red Bluff, California. The callsign was "Mercy."

Hands-on

F-16 training by the FTD at Hill was initiated on July 1. The first two pilots reported to Luke AFB on September 20 for F-16 training. The first Fighting Falcon, F-16A 80070, was taxied from the 388th ramp to the 419th TFW ramp on October 16 by Lt Col James Fauske, who was the 419th TFW's TAC advisor. The initial two F-16s were used by the FTD for hands-on training and limited flying training.

In the final full six months that the 419th TFW flew the Thunderchief, 1,192 sorties were scheduled and 1,002 flown. As to flying hours the numbers were 1,765 and 1,327, respectively. Deviations from the flying schedule were caused for instance by weather, and hydraulic and control systems deficiencies. It became necessary to obtain parts from retired F-105s at MASDC.

After the June 4 flyby, the first six of ultimately ten F-105Ds were flown to Kelly AFB, Texas. From there they were towed to the AFMTC at Lackland for use in the training program of security policemen in securing a flight line. The photo shows the flight line with ten inactive Thunderchiefs, all in excellent condition. (TvG)

In a January 11, 1984, message, AFRes informed the 419th TFW at Hill that AFLC AAD 84-187 reassigned seven F-105Ds from the Wing to the Air Force Museum under Project AFM 3F-086. The aircraft were to be delivered to various bases for static display purposes. One of the aircraft involved was 24361. It proved to be the final operational F-105D to be phased out of USAF's inventory. On February 9, 1984, Maj O.C. Hope flew "361" to Port Columbus Airport, Ohio for display at the Defense Construction Supply Center. The May 1983 photo shows 361 at Gulfport ANG Training Site, Mississippi prior to a sortie in Fighter Comp 83. (Norm Taylor)

The formal conversion from the F-105 to the F-16 was initiated on January 1, 1984. In that month, eight F-105Ds departed the 419th. During the UTA on January 28–29, the first F-16 was formally accepted. On February 9, there were four F-105Fs and nine F-16A/Bs assigned. Two of the F-105Fs participated on February 17–18 in a joint maritime operation at NAS Lemoore, California. On February 24, F-105F 38365 departed for the Oklahoma City Air Logistics Center at Tinker AFB, where it would be used in the Aircraft Battle Damage Repair (ABDR) program.

Dedicated

The phase-out of the final three Thunderchiefs took place at Hill on February 25 during the "Thud Out," "A historic event commemorating the final flight of the F-105 Thunderchief," according to the cover of the invitation. Its theme was, "People, Let Me Tell Ya 'Bout My Best Friend." The last official mission began at 10:45L. The callsign was "Thud." Thud 01/38287 was Lt Col Jim Webster (135 F-105 combat sorties and 3,000 F-105 flying hours, ranking sixth among all F-105 pilots) with Col Tom Coady (commander of the 475th Weapons Evaluation Group at Tyndall AFB, Florida, with over 1,000 combat hours in the F-105, the most of any F-105 pilot). Thud 02/38261 was Maj Frank Bernard (one of four F-105D pilots to fly the last F-105D combat mission of the Vietnam War on October 6, 1970) with Col Merlyn Dethlefsen (Medal of Honor). Thud 03/38309 was Maj Barry Wyttenbach (180 F-105 combat sorties) and Col Leo Thorsness.

While the three F-105Fs were in the air, they were refueled by KC-135E 71422 of the 931st Air Refueling Group (Grissom AFB, Indiana). The Stratotanker hosted a group of people who were busy taking photographs during the refueling activities. In the meantime, BG Roger Scheer, Deputy to the Chief, Air Force Reserve and long-time F-105 pilot with 3,493.3 hours (ranking third), dedicated F-105D 24347, the high-time F-105 with 6,730.5 flying hours, on a pedestal to all who lost their life flying the F-105. At that moment the three two-seaters performed a missing man flyover. The initial plan was for the F-105Fs to land at Davis-Monthan for storage with the crews being returned to Hill by airlift. However, on February 10, USAF approved the aircraft to return to Hill and to be flown to various museums later.

Banquet

Some 1,500 people attended an open house with around 20 aircraft on display, most of them having been flown in by former F-105 pilots. In the evening, the 466th TFS sponsored the Thud Out banquet in the Wing's hangar. It was attended by 500 people. In attendance were, among others, eight former POWs; the first F-105 pilot to down a North Vietnamese MiG, Lt Col Fred Tracy; and the F-105 pilot with the most flying hours (3,709.6), Col Ray Kingston. The keynote speaker was Col Thorsness, with several other people also speaking. The first one, Theo van Geffen, gave an oversight of the F-105's history, supported by SMSgt Jerry Arruda behind the slide projector. He was followed by, among others, Col Bob Scott (commander of the first F-105 squadron who claimed a MiG-17 on March 26, 1967, as commander of the 355th TFW at Takhli RTAB); Hank Beaird (who, on May 16, 1956, made the first F-105B flight at Edwards AFB. However, the flight did not end as advertised, as the nose gear did not extend, forcing Beaird to make a wheels-up landing, which resulted in minor damage); MSgt Wally Craggs, a 14-year veteran crew chief; and Robert Sanator, President of Fairchild Republic. Capt Randy Stallard of the 465th TFS wrote the final tribute song, *So Long F-105*. A special Thud Out patch was designed. TAC published *TAC News Service*, and with regard to the Thud Out, it issued TAC-84-46, "The F-105 honored in retirement ceremony." It began as follows, "If they gave Oscars for airplane retirements, the F-105 Thunderchief would have won them all: showmanship, nostalgia, best song, script, and musical score."

Three to go

The "fate" of the three F-105Fs was as follows: On February 27, the first aircraft to depart, 38309, was flown solo by Jim Webster to Robins AFB, Georgia, for ABDR training by the 2955th Combat Logistics Support Squadron (CLSS). It was scrapped in July 1995. The second aircraft, 38261, followed on March 3 with callsign "Regma 11." It was flown by Maj Kent Clark and Theo van Geffen to Little Rock AFB, Arkansas, to go on static display at the All Flags Heritage Park at Camp Robinson. This sortie proved to be the final two-person sortie of the F-105. On November 24, 2008, "261" was trucked to the Museum of Military History in Jacksonville, Arkansas. Col Thorsness was the speaker when the aircraft was dedicated on September 25, 2009.

F-105F 38287 and F-16A 80070 of the 466th TFS on a low approach at Hill on February 24, 1984, with the snow-covered Wasatch mountain range as a backdrop. (TvG)

USAF's final three Thunderchiefs on Hill's runway just seconds prior to their final operational mission. (TvG)

The third F-105F, 38287, was flown by Capt Joe Gelinger as Thud 01 to Chanute AFB, Illinois, to go on display at its Aerospace Museum. As Chanute did not have an active runway, it was decided to leave the rear seat empty. Gellinger said:

I was supposed to deliver "287" on March 9, but a big snowstorm had hit Chanute on the 8th and closed the field. As the 6,301ft runway had been inactivated with no overruns, barriers, and tower, I needed to make sure the runway was clear and dry. On the morning of March 10, Chanute advised me that the field was clear, and they wanted the airplane that day. The weather looked good, so I headed out. It was a little long for one hop, so I landed at Offutt AFB, Nebraska, for gas. The weather at Chanute was still clear and I took off. Since Champaign, 15 miles to the south of Chanute, was my alternate, I decided to shoot a practice approach there just in case I could not land at Chanute. When I got about 50 miles out, the weather sure did not look clear and when I inquired, it was partially obscured at Champaign, one mile visibility and snow. I shot the approach in bad weather and then took a radar vector north to Chanute. To my relief, the weather had cleared up some to about 2,500 feet overcast and three miles visibility. I visually picked up Chanute and for 15 minutes really "heated up" the field, doing high speed passes and some practice approaches. When I had 2,000 pounds of gas left, it was time to land. I was concerned about stopping on such a short runway, but the book said an F model could be stopped in 2,400 feet with the chute and 4,900 feet without it, but with maximum breaking. I made a shallow approach, flew it very slow, touched down 300 feet from the runway's end, had a 20 knot headwind, immediately deployed the drag chute and got on the brakes. At 13:05L on March 10, 1984, it was a sad time and the last landing of a great airplane. It was a great honor for me to be allowed to make that final flight.

Although the museum remained open after Chanute was closed on September 30, 1993, a lack of operating funds resulted in the decision to scrap "287" and seven other aircraft. The aircraft were sold in September 2017.

Of the six ANG and three AFRes squadrons that flew the Thunderchief, the 466th TFS was the only Squadron to fly both the B and D/F models. While flying the F-105B, the unit also had AT/T-33 aircraft assigned. In 31,092 sorties, the Diamondback collected 43,369 flying hours. Three aircraft were lost over the years: two B and one D model.

With the next to last of the three remaining F-105Fs, 38261, the final full crew sortie ever with the type was flown on March 3, as Regma 11, to Little Rock AFB. In the photo are its two crew members and crew chiefs Scott Fickett and Kent Clayton. (TvG)

The final ever F-105 Thunderchief flight took place on March 10 when Capt Joe Gelinger flew 38287 as Thud 01 to Chanute AFB. As the base did not have an active runway, it was decided to leave the rear seat empty. (Joe Gelinger)

Chapter 10

Air National Guard and Air Force Reserve in Pictures

The 119th TFS at Atlantic City Airport, New Jersey, was the ANG unit that flew the F-105 for the shortest period; in June 1970 the conversion from the F-100C/F to the F-105B was initiated, while on January 27, 1973, the squadron was re-designated 119th FIS after conversion to the F-106A/B Delta Dart. The photo shows 119th TFS F-105B 75838 taxiing at Kelly AFB in March 1972. (Norm Taylor)

The 121st TFS of the District of Columbia ANG (DCANG) at Andrews AFB, Maryland, received the first two of 26 F-105D/Fs on June 1, 1971, converting from F-100C/Fs. While converting to the F-4D Phantom, the unit's final F-105, D/10056, departed on February 12, 1982. F-105D 10041 on last chance prior to a training sortie from Andrews. (TvG)

All F-105D units also had F-105F two-seaters assigned. F-105F 24433 of the DCANG returns to Andrews after a training mission. (TvG)

The first Pave Spike-configured F-4D, 67693, arrived at Andrews on June 13, 1980. (TvG)

With the 23rd TFW being collocated at McConnell, it was not surprising the 127th TFS became the F-105 schoolhouse, resulting in a re-designation to TFTS. The unit traded in its F-100C/Fs. On January 21, 1971, the first two F-105s were taxied across the base from the 23rd TFW flight line. The 127th TFTS converted to the F-4D. (TvG)

F-105Ds 24299 and 24347 were the last two Thunderchiefs to depart the 127th TFTS and McConnell on March 28, 1980, both being reassigned to the 466th TFS at Hill. (TvG)

Above: As the F-105 schoolhouse, the 127th TFTS possessed as many as six F-105F two-seaters. Here, 24417 taxies out for a training sortie. (TvG)

Below: The two T-39Bs were used by the 127th to give F-105 pilots the required radar familiarization training, radar navigation, and radarscope interpretation. Both aircraft were transferred to the 4950th Test Wing. (TvG)

The 128th TFS at Dobbins AFB, Georgia, was the sixth ANG unit converting to the F-105 (from the F-100D/F). It was the only unit to receive F-105G Wild Weasel aircraft. The first aircraft, F-105G 24428, arrived on September 13, 1978. The 128th converted to F-4Ds as well. The final F-105, F/38299, was flown on May 25, 1983, by Maj Duff Greene to NAS Patuxent River, Maryland. The photo shows weapon technicians reloading the Vulcan cannon of F-105G 38363. (TvG)

Right: F-105G 24439 prior to entering the runway. Note the empty back seat and the VMA-513/AV-8 stencil. (TvG)

Below: Three F-105Gs being refueled by a KC-135A Stratotanker prior to flying a mission at the Avon Park Range, Florida. (TvG)

Two F-105Gs in the break for the landing at Dobbins AFB. (TvG)

A total of six ANG Tactical Fighter Squadrons converted to the F-105 Thunderchief, two to the B model, and four to the D/F model. The first unit to convert from F-84Fs to F-105Bs was the 141st TFS at McGuire AFB, New Jersey, with it formally accepting its first aircraft, 75776, on April 16, 1964. On May 6, 1981, the F-105B phase-out was completed while converting to the F-4D. (via Norm Taylor)

The 141st TFS was the only ANG unit flying non-camouflaged Thunderchiefs. The last of the 21 F-105Bs was received in December 1968 and included four ex-Thunderbirds aircraft. The May 1965 photo shows the flight line at McGuire. (Coll/TvG)

August 18–25, 1968, the 141st participated with 11 F-105Bs from Tanagra AB, Greece, in NATO's annual field training exercise, *Deep Furrow 1-68*. Of the 149 sorties scheduled, 148 were flown for a total of 404 flying hours. In the photo, three of the participating F-105Bs are on last chance at McGuire before departure. (USAF)

Above: The 149th TFS at Byrd Field, Virginia, was the second and final ANG unit converting to the F-105 from F-84F Thunderstreaks. It received its first F-105, a D model, on January 19, 1971, beating the 127th TFS by two days. It also became the only ANG F-105 unit to convert to the A-7D Corsair II. The final four F-105s, all Fs, were transferred in November 1981. The October 23, 1976, photo shows F-105D/Fs of the 149th TFS on their *Coronet Fife* deployment to RAF Lakenheath. (Ken Keeton)

Right: On April 27, 1979, the author flew an F-105F sortie with the 149th TFS in 24413. Most, if not all, unit F-105D/Fs had been adorned with artwork accomplished by TSgt Beetle Bailey. For this occasion, he adorned "413" with "The Flying Dutchman" artwork. The photo shows Bailey (L), pilot Capt Bill Campenni (M), and crew chief, SSgt Leon Brooks (R). (TvG)

F-105F 24413 during the April 27, 1979, mission. (Don Spering/AIR)

Two 149th TFS F-105Ds on a low approach to Byrd Field after a mission to Fort Bragg. (TvG)

When the F-105 made its entry into Air Force Reserve units at Carswell, Tinker, and Hill, the units had C-124 Globemasters assigned, meaning build-up was to be from scratch. The first Carswell F-105, D/10100, was flown in by Lt Col Bob Johnston of the 23rd TFW from McConnell on May 10, 1972, after which the aircraft was christened *The City of Fort Worth II* by Miss Fort Worth, Debra Kinler. It was assigned to the 916th Military Airlift Group (MAG) until July 8, 1972, when the 457th TFS was activated in the Reserve. The photo shows F-105D 10100 after its arrival. (USAF)

The Thunderstick II F-105Ds of the 457th were all received from the 563rd TFS at McConnell. 00471 was the F-105D assigned to the 301st TFW commander and on the tail and radar reflector carried the three colors of the Wing's three fighter squadrons: red for the 457th, blue for the 465th, and yellow for the 466th TFS. The 457th TFS converted to Pave Spike/LORAN-configured F-4Ds with the last three F-105s leaving on February 26, 1982. (TvG)

Right: One of the F-105Fs of the 457th TFS, 38261, at Carswell. (TvG)

Below: In the August 12–27, 1977, period, 14 aircraft of the 457th, including D/00500 and four of the 465th TFS, deployed to Nörvenich AB, Germany, to participate in *Coronet Poker*. The deployment was the first time an AFRes fighter unit deployed to an Allied operating base. (Coll/TvG)

In April 1972, the USAF announced that the 937th MAG at Tinker would convert to F-105D/Fs rather than C-130s, as had been scheduled previously. It had been nearly 15 years since any AFRes unit had a tactical fighter mission. Until activation in the Reserve of the 465th TFS (May 20, 1972), the arriving F-105s (the first arrived on May 10) were assigned to the 937th MAG. Also on May 20, the 465th was assigned to the 507th TFG, while this group was assigned to the 442nd Tactical Airlift Wing. The 442nd had two C-130 units with tail codes "UA" and "UB." When the 465th TFS joined, its tail code became "UC." F-105D 24284 was a triple MiG killer, but unfortunately it crashed on March 12, 1976, killing the pilot. (TvG)

Above: F-105F 38365 taxiing out for a training sortie. The 465th TFS became the first AFRes unit to convert to F-4Ds. The F-105's final sortie was flown on December 11, 1980, when Lt Col Durnbaugh flew D/00514 to Carswell. (TvG)

Left: After the unit had, surprisingly, received permission to do so, the tail code "UC" was changed to "SH" in October 1974. The photo shows three "SH"-coded F-105Ds on last chance. (TvG)

On July 19, 1979, F-105D 24372 became the very first F-105 to surpass 6,000 flying hours. The pilot was Capt Randy Freeman, and the aircraft's crew chief was TSgt Melvin Morrow. The aircraft was delivered to the USAF on September 13, 1963. It was one of the first three F-105s to be assigned to Tinker with 4,390 hours on the clock. Both in 1976 and 1978 it earned the High Flyer of the Year Award, flying 288.7 and 300.5 hours, respectively. When the 465th converted to F-4Ds, "372" was reassigned to the 466th TFS at Hill. (USAF)

The 945th MAG at Hill was the third AFRes C-124C unit to convert to F-105s. However, it received the F-105Bs of the 119th TFS. Only one C-124 pilot, Capt Glen Jepsen, would transition to the F-105. Although the 466th Strategic Fighter Squadron had been re-designated on June 23, 1972, as a TFS, it lasted until January 1, 1973, when the unit was activated with subsequent inactivation of the airlift infrastructure. The final Globemaster departed Hill on November 27, 1972, at which time the 945th had eight F-105Bs and five AT-33A trainers. To mark the event, a flyover was made by a C-124C, AT-33A, and F-105B. The 466th TFS made two F-105B deployments to NAS Barbers Point, Hawaii: *Coronet Crane* in January 1978, and *Coronet Intake/Paid-Lei* in January 1980. The second deployment included an ORI. The photo shows three F-105Bs in the company of two TA-4J Skyhawks of Fleet Composite Squadron (VC) One, stationed at Barbers Point. The final F-105B sortie was flown on January 5, 1981, when Maj Jim Caldwell flew 75838 to Volk Field, Wisconsin, for static display. Six days earlier, the final T-33A had departed Hill. (USN)

Operation *Rattler* was initiated by the 466th TFS in the fall of 1978 to enhance the CR proficiency of F-105 pilots of the 301st TFW. In addition to the three 301st units, several other units deployed to Hill to participate in the 2–3-day events, which included air-to-ground and dissimilar aircraft combat training missions at the Utah Test and Training Range (UTTR). The largest and most memorable *Rattler* was held on November 3–4, 1979. The unit's history stated that "it was the largest single gathering of F-105s since Southeast Asia with 60 F-105B/D/F/Gs participating of seven different units." Other units included the 555th TFTS (F-15A), 310th TFTS (F-4C), and VMFA-314 (F-4J). The history also stated the following: "Reportedly, F-105 aircrews, employing terrain masking tactics and flying low and fast, were so successful, not a single F-105 was detected by the opposition's F-4/F-15 air defense force." (USAF)

By December 31, 1980, all F-105D/Fs had been received at Hill. In 1982, the 466th TFS had F-105Ds in different color schemes, like this wrap-around camouflaged 24301, "My Karma." (TvG)

F-105D 24299 was painted in desert camouflage. (TvG)

Three F-105Ds of the 466th TFS with extended speed brakes on an October 15, 1982, mission over the Great Salt Lake, Utah. (TvG)

August 12–30, 1981, the 466th TFS deployed with 18 F-105s (17D/1F) and 387 personnel to Skrydstrup AB, Denmark as *Coronet Rudder*. The unit participated in Exercise *Oksboel 81* with NATO forces and in the Royal Danish Air Force's annual fighter weaponry competition. On August 26, 1st Lt Dennis Mason became the only pilot of the 466th TFS to get lost in the line of duty while the unit flew the F-105. On that day, he was the number four in a four-ship CAS mission to Oksboel Range. Shortly after entering the low fighter engagement zone, over rough ocean north of the Jutland peninsula to practice defensive lookout training, an F-5E aggressor pilot made a "knock it off" call because of an observed fireball/explosion. The fireball was F-105D 24372. No trace of the pilot and aircraft was found. The photo shows "372" at Skrydstrup prior to its loss. By that time, it had accumulated some 6,500 flying hours. (Coll/TvG)